Your Master's Thesis

Studymates

British History 1870–1918
Warfare 1792–1918
Hitler and Nazi Germany (3rd Edition)
English Reformation
European History 1870–1918
Genetics (2nd edition)
Lenin, Stalin and Communist Russia
Organic Chemistry (2nd Edition)
Chemistry: As Chemistry Explained
Chemistry: Chemistry Calculations Explained
The New Science Teacher's Handbook
Mathematics for Adults
Calculus
Understanding Forces
Algebra: Basic Algebra Explained
Plant Physiology
Poems to Live By
Shakespeare
Poetry
Better English
Better French
Better German
Better Spanish
Social Anthropology
Statistics for Social Science
Practical Drama
The War Poets 1914–18
The Academic Essay
Your Master's Thesis
Your PhD Thesis

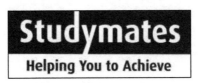

Your Master's Thesis

**Edited by
Alan Bond**

www.studymates.co.uk

Contents

Acknowledgements   vii

Biographical information   ix

1. Planning and organising a master's thesis   **1**
Chris Harding

2. Understanding the Role of Theory   **17**
Colin Wight

3. Constructing and Interpreting Qualitative Data   **29**
Mark Goodwin

4. Analysing Quantitative Data   **51**
Alan Bond, John Brierley and Mark Tippett

5. Getting Down to Brass Tacks: The Hard Graft of Writing   **67**
Norma Green

6. Legal and moral issues   **85**
Allison Coleman and John Williams

7. Understanding Submission and Examination Processes   **99**
Gina Preston

8. Explaining how to Publish   **113**
Alan Bond

Glossary   **125**

Index   **133**

Acknowledgements

The original impetus for this book came from the fact that, while director of an MSc programme by distance-learning at the University of Wales Aberystwyth, it was clear that there was a very real problem in communicating to students, who were based at a distance, just what might be expected in a Master's dissertation.

In fact, it also seemed to be the case that for full-time Master's students, there was an often-unwarranted assumption (on behalf of the academics involved) that the knowledge of what was expected and how tasks might be undertaken was greater than it should have been. Initial attempts to address the problem for the distance-learning students led to the development of a 'thesis school', which students attended before starting their Master's research. Feedback from the school was excellent, and publishing the same sort of advice handed out at that school seemed too great an opportunity to miss.

Early planning of the book, then, revolved around all the questions that Master's students might ask at stages before embarking on their research until after they had submitted. Selecting appropriate members of staff to cover the diversity of advice needed was actually very easy in a university environment and I had been fortunate to have many colleagues give up their time for free – often at weekends – to provide input to the 'thesis school'.

However, it was then that the first mistake was made – I hope the co-authors will forgive this ...! To increase credibility, the authors selected were invariably at the top of their field – but these are very busy people and getting copy from them, bearing in mind the already oversubscribed nature of their diaries, proved difficult. So while some authors laboured, others had to wait. Editing some chapters also ruffled feathers because I have many years of experience of producing distance-learning materials where readability is all-important and split infinitives and other grammatical horrors are more-or-less ignored in such a context (or even embraced in their place).

Through all this, as each chapter finally surfaced, my belief that this guide would be useful to all those who read it has made it worth the wait. I'm very happy with the result and am very grateful to all the authors for putting up with my assassination of their writing style.

To you, the reader, I make a promise. I have assembled a truly professional team and they have delivered what is, in my judgement, superb advice for any student. Read what they have to say, listen to their voices, learn from their experience and you too will achieve your goal of writing your Master's thesis.

Between them, the authors have experience of working in many universities, although when the project started all were at the same establishment. I believe that this wealth of experience of different university environments means that this book provides advice that is universally applicable.

Alan Bond – Editor

Biographical information

Alan Bond (PhD) is a senior lecturer specialising in environmental impact assessment in the School of Environmental Sciences, University of East Anglia. Previously he was course director for the distance-learning MSc in Environmental Impact Assessment at the University of Wales, Aberystwyth where he wrote eight 150 page modules. He is author of *Environmental Assessment in the UK* (Chandos Press, 2000) and a member of the editorial board of *Environmental Impact Assessment Review* and *Impact Assessment and Project Appraisal* (IAPA).

Chris Harding is a Professor of Law, and was Director of Postgraduate Studies for UWA from 1995 to 1998; teaching at Aberystwyth since 1973. Recent publications are *Regulating Cartels in Europe* with Julian Joshua (Oxford University Press, 2003); *Renegotiating Westphalia: Essays and Commentary on the European and Theoretical Foundations of Modern International Law*, co-editor with C.L. Lim and contributor of two papers therein (Matinus Nijhoff, 1999); and *Diversion in the Criminal Process* with Gavin Dingwall (Sweet & Maxwell, 1998).

Colin Wight is a senior lecturer in the Department of International Politics, The University of Wales Aberystwyth. His research interests are in the interface between the philosophy of social science, social theory and international relations theory. He is currently researching the role played by the 'Idea of Science' in the formation of international relations as an academic discipline. He has published in the *Philosophy of the Social Sciences*, *International Studies Quarterly*, *European Journal of International Relations* and *Millennium*. He is currently working on a book dealing with social ontologies of international politics.

Mark Goodwin is Professor of Human Geography at the University of Exeter, and Director of Research for the School of Geography, Archaeology and Earth Resources. Previously he was Director of the Institute of Geography and Earth Sciences at the University of Wales Aberystwyth where he was also Director of Postgraduate Studies for the University. He is the joint author of *Practising Human Geography* (Sage, 2004), which explores the construction and interpretation of geographical data, and joint editor of *Introducing Human Geographies* (Hodder Arnold, 2005) and *Envisioning Human Geographies* (Hodder Arnold, 2004).

John Brierley is a lecturer in accounting and finance at the University of Sheffield. He has worked previously at the University of Manchester and the University of Wales Aberystwyth. His current research interest is in the area of product costing.

Professor Mark Tippett (PhD; C.A. (Australia)) is a chartered accountant and Professor of Accounting at Loughborough University. He is immediate past joint editor of *British Accounting Review* and a member of the editorial board for the *Journal of Business Finance and Accounting*.

Norma Green (MA) was Director of Programmes, English Language Unit (now called the Language and Learning Centre) at the University of Wales Aberystwyth, retiring in 1998. Norma has taught writing techniques and English language for over 25 years in the University of Wales Aberystwyth, the University of Malawi and in the United States. She also trained students on the PGCE (UWA) course, and acted as consultant to the University of Malawi and Universitas Bengkulu (Sumatra). She has edited numerous Master's and PhD theses, as well as scientific books and learned papers. Her contributions to *New Ways in Teaching Writing*, ed. R.V. White, University of Reading (TESOL, 1995) were developed from her classroom and tutorial experience.

John Williams is Barrister-at-Law, and Professor of Law at the University of Wales Aberystwyth. He has published a number of books, the more recent ones including *Social Services Law* (2nd edition) (Tolley, 1995); *How to Keep a Clinical Confidence* (HMSO, 1994) with B. Darley, A. Griew & K. McLaughlin; 'Community Care: the Law and Rural Areas' in *Legal Provision in the Rural Environment*, eds. C. Harding & J. Williams (University of Wales Press, 1994); 'Open Adoption – the Way Foward' in *Social Policy Crime & Punishment*, eds. I.G. Jones & G. Williams (University of Wales Press, 1994); 'The Use of an Expert System to present the Mental Health Act to Social Workers' with R. Hartley & S. Morris in *Computers and Law*, eds. I. Carr & K.S. Williams (Intellect Books, 1994); and 'Child Protection and the Criminal Justice System' in *The Child Protection Handbook*, eds. K. Wilson & A. James (Balliere Tindall, London, 2002).

Allison Coleman (LLM) is a freelance copyright consultant. She was for many years a senior lecturer in Law at the University of Wales Aberystwyth, then chief executive of two digital content companies. She is the author of *The Legal Protection of Trade Secrets* (Sweet and Maxwell, 1992); *Intellectual Property Law* (Longman: Law, Tax and Finance, 1994); *Professional Issues in Software Engineering* (3rd edition) with Bott, Eaton and Rowland (Taylor and Francis, 2001); and *Copyright Exceptions – the Digital Impact* with Burrell (Cambridge University Press, 2005).

Gina Preston was postgraduate admissions officer for the University of Wales Aberystwyth from July 1993 until March 2003. She had responsibility for the administration of all applications for postgraduate study at the university. The postgraduate admissions office is part of the university's admissions and recruitment office, and she was in charge of policy relating to the recruitment of postgraduate students and the marketing of programmes and courses of postgraduate study.

Contact details

Dr Alan Bond

InteREAM (Interdisciplinary Research in Environmental Assessment and Management)

School of Environmental Sciences

University of East Anglia

Norwich, NR4 7TJ

Tel. 01603 593402

Fax. 01603 591327

Email: alan.bond@uea.ac.uk; zwk@aber.ac.uk

Skype name: inteream

Web: http://www.uea.ac.uk/env/inteream/

Allison Coleman,

C/o Dr Alan Bond

Email: aic@aber.ac.uk; allison_coleman@btinternet.com

Christopher Harding,

Department of Law

University of Wales

Penglais,

Aberystwyth, SY23 3DY

Tel: 01970 622734

Fax: 01970 622729

Email: csh@aber.ac.uk

Professor John Williams

Department of Law

University of Wales

Aberystwyth, SY23 3DB

Tel: 01970 622735

Fax: 01970 621540

Email: jow@aber.ac.uk

Professor Mark Goodwin

Department of Geography

SoGAER

University of Exeter

Amory Building

Rennes Drive

Exeter, EX4 4RJ

Tel: 01392 262439

Fax: 01392 263342

Email: M.Goodwin@exeter.ac.uk

John A. Brierley

Sheffield University Management School

9 Mappin Street

The University of Sheffield

Sheffield, S1 4DT

Email: J.A.Brierley@sheffield.ac.uk

Professor Mark Tippett

Professor of Accounting and Finance

The Business School

Loughborough University

Ashby Road

Loughborough, LE11 3TU

Email: M.Tippett@lboro.ac.uk

Norma Green

C/o Dr Alan Bond

Email: nog_green@yahoo.co.uk

Gina Preston

C/o Dr Alan Bond

Email: ginavpreston@yahoo.co.uk

Dr Colin Wight

Department of Politics

University of Sheffield

Elmfield

Northumberland Road

Sheffield, S10 2TU

Email: C.Wight@sheffield.ac.uk

1 Planning and Organising a Master's Thesis

Chris Harding

One-minute overview

This chapter will consider the objectives and scope of a Master's thesis and the process of designing and organising the research necessary to produce such a thesis. It will also examine the supervisory relationship, so as to indicate the level of assistance and guidance which may be expected from a supervisor.

The following main issues will be discussed:

■ introducing the objectives in completing a Master's thesis;

■ choosing the subject for research;

■ planning and managing your time;

■ designing your research;

■ working with your supervisor;

■ case studies;

■ discussion points;

■ questions and answers.

Introducing the objectives in completing a master's thesis

Writing a thesis is an exercise in carrying out research and writing up an account of that research activity. If you have not completed a research dissertation as part of your undergraduate course, this may be your first experience of a sustained research exercise. Since a Master's thesis is part of a postgraduate scheme of study, more will be expected of you compared to the kind of assignment you would usually have been given as an undergraduate.

Firstly, the scale of the activity is likely to be much larger. Typically, work on a Master's thesis will comprise about one third of the time and effort within your degree scheme – usually a period of three or four months' work after the taught part of the programme has been completed. If your university uses a credit system, it is likely that 60 credits will be assigned to the thesis component of the degree, out of a total of 180 credits for one year of postgraduate study. Most degree regulations will specify that the thesis should be between 15,000 and 20,000 words in length. All of this should provide you with some idea of the amount of work involved in the thesis. To put this into context, if you double-space your work you should probably expect to produce about a 50-page document, depending on the nature of the research and any diagrams included.

Secondly, there is a qualitative difference between a Master's thesis and a typical undergraduate essay. As an undergraduate, the titles and subjects of your written work will usually have been set for you. As a postgraduate, you will be expected to select an appropriate topic for research yourself, which will then be approved by your supervisor and department. You will also be expected to probe the subject further and to use more sophisticated research methodology. In short, your role will be much more of an independent one.

It may be helpful to locate your Master's thesis in an educational context. On the one hand, it will involve a more substantial exercise in research and academic writing compared to your undergraduate experience. On the other hand, less will be expected of you, concerning both the scale and level of the work, compared to the requirements of a full postgraduate research degree (either MPhil or PhD). Viewed in this way, the Master's thesis provides a bridge between the 'taught' element in higher education, and study through independent research activity. You can thus see your work on the thesis as a short period of apprenticeship in research activity, or the first stage in developing crucial generic research skills – in particular, those of identifying a worthwhile research topic, planning research and organising time, locating and using research data, and organising and writing an account of the research.

Choosing the subject for research

As this is an exercise in independent research, your first task will be to identify an appropriate subject to be covered in a Master's thesis. To be able to do this you will need to be familiar with your wider field of study and you will need an ability to identify, from your earlier study of the subject, interesting and significant questions that merit further enquiry or discussion. For many students, especially those just embarking on research activity, this may be one of the most difficult parts of the whole exercise. What is worthwhile in research terms is unlikely to be as obvious to the relative novice as to the seasoned academic researcher. This is not something to worry about, however, as the supervisor's role is to provide just this sort of advice.

You may well already have developed ideas about possible research topics during the earlier part of your course – seminar discussions or written assignments may have raised unresolved points of interest and triggered the suggestion of further enquiry. For example, a science student may have discussed the perception that an oil spill has brought a particular species of sea bird close to extinction. As this was a perception, and there were no actual facts to back it up, you might decide that it was a worthy topic for investigation. However, remember that while the choice of subject for research should be essentially your decision, you will be expected to take the opportunity to discuss possibilities with your supervisor, and perhaps other staff if appropriate – and in any case you will not be allowed to proceed with a project which is academically worthless or unworkable. Thus your choice of subject will be made subject to guidance and advice. Taking the same example, it may be that you discuss this idea with your supervisor, who then refers you to recently published research that answers the questions you were hoping to investigate in your thesis. While disappointing, this discussion has saved you a lot of time!

There are both academic and practical considerations you should bear in mind when choosing a subject for research. In academic terms, the subject should comprise problems of significance and/or a topic that has not received very much attention, as yet, so that there are genuine questions which have not been fully or satisfactorily answered, or material which has not been extensively studied. You may be advised, for instance, that a subject 'has been done to death' or that 'this is a well trodden path', implying that there is little which would be new to say about the subject, and that it would not therefore be appropriate to write your thesis on this same subject.

In practical terms there will necessarily be limits as regards what you will be able to achieve within a period of a few months. An awareness of the time and resources actually at your disposal should constrain your choice of subject, and remember that it is a good idea to ask your supervisor at an early stage for an opinion on your research plan to get an early warning about overambitious plans which cannot be completed by the deadline. Your choice of subject should, therefore, be informed by a number of basic questions. These are illustrated in Figure 1 and are explained in more detail below.

● Does the subject raise genuine and interesting questions – is it worthwhile?

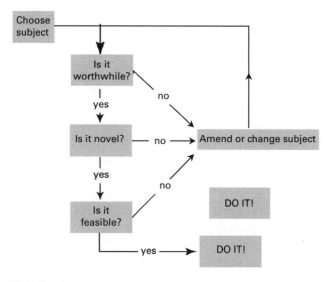

Fig. 1: Choosing your subject

- To what extent has the ground been covered by other researchers – is it novel?
- Can the subject be covered adequately, in terms of being researched and written up, in the time available – is it feasible?

The other important point to bear in mind is that there is limited time available for the purposes of making this initial, but crucial, decision. In practice, some Master's students are able to give the question some thought at an earlier point in the course, for instance when ideas first occur to them, by discussing the suitability and potential of the subject with academic staff in advance of the date for starting work properly on the thesis. It may well be an advantage, then, to give the matter some preliminary thought earlier on. In any event, avoid getting bogged down in choosing a topic at the beginning of the research period. Although good supervisors will be alert to this danger, you cannot rely on a supervisor continually chasing you to get started.

Planning and managing your time

In any programme of research, an appreciation of the timescale of the project is essential. In the case of a thesis, the timescale is defined for you by the starting and submission dates (for instance, June – when the taught part of the programme is completed, to start – and end of September – for submission). It is worth noting that some universities' regulations allow a longer period before the submission deadline, but a timescale of three months is widely recognised as being adequate and, unless there are good reasons, potential employers may question why it has taken longer. Having fixed dates at least provides you with a frame for a timetable and you should then consider (again, often in consultation with the supervisor) how much of the time available you should allocate to the key phases of your research and writing up. Much will, of course, depend on the more precise subject of the research and such matters as the availability of materials and the method being used to collect data.

Remember that there are two main types of activity involved in the production of any kind of thesis – the research and the writing-up. You certainly need to consider the proportion of available time needed for each of these key tasks and take care in the early stages not to be over-optimistic about the speed at which you can write up the results of your research in an organised and lucid form. Writing up often takes longer than most researchers wish or expect, especially the technical aspects of the process such as referencing and producing tables, diagrams or other special types of format.

Ideally you should have a clear and realistic timetable, checked and approved by your supervisor, worked out as soon as possible. This can then help to give you some sense of where you are going and at what speed.

Designing your research

In some ways, the conventional format of a research thesis in itself supplies a structure within which to define your research effort. A glance at a number of completed theses will reveal that they are usually laid out in a series of more or less uniform stages:

- an introductory section which explains the scope, objectives and methods of the research, and provides some background information and a statement on existing literature on the subject by way of supplying context;
- a main section reporting on the research;
- a concluding section summarising and discussing the research outcomes.

You may feel constrained by the conventions of style and presentation but, in effect, they tell you how to lay out the thesis in broad terms. Obviously, rules or recommendations as to the length of the thesis will immediately determine the size and scope of the research. But also bear in mind that the production of a thesis is a self-contained research exercise with an educational point – to prove and judge your ability in carrying out and writing about research. Therefore, you will be expected to produce the thesis in a certain format.

The research exercise is called a 'thesis' for a particular reason. The word means 'argument' and it is expected that you will not just carry out research in the sense of uncovering a subject (what you might call the 'spadework') but that you will also demonstrate that there is point to what you are doing – that it has some value in terms of improving knowledge and understanding of the subject. This process of showing the academic worth of your work will, in practice, comprise the argument of your thesis. It is always useful to remember the distinction between good academic work, which should have some value for society, and more personally motivated research, which is usually described as a 'hobby'. Most people have personal interests which may be fascinating for them as individuals, but not necessarily of significance or value to others. It is part of the rigour of academic research that it requires a justification over and above mere personal interest, and one of the elements of the argument you should present in your thesis is the reason why your chosen topic and line of enquiry is of wider value.

This process of demonstrating the value of your research and, in doing so constructing an argument, may be summarised by posing some very basic questions, which should be addressed in designing any research activity which is intended to be of value to the rest of the world. Figure 2 details these basic questions in flow chart form and suggests an order for approaching them.

In practice, you should already have considered these questions in choosing your subject and in judging the value and feasibility of the proposed topic. The 'what' and 'why' questions should help you to assess the inherent research value of your subject; the 'how' question should enable you to determine whether, and in what way, the research may be accomplished within the limits of your time and resources.

Having a clear idea of these questions at the beginning is not only essential for the purposes of choosing a viable and worthwhile subject to research, but is also very useful in allowing you to map out the shape and direction of your research over the coming months. It provides you with valuable signposts to enable you to keep to the route that you

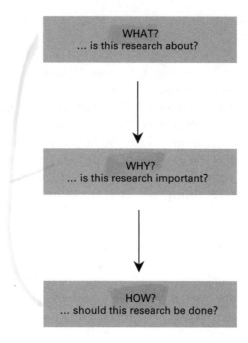

Fig. 2: Designing your research

have set for yourself, by acting as a reminder of your objectives and methods. Your plan or design thus serves as an aide-memoire as you progress with your project so that you can remind yourself:

- What is the scope and what are the boundaries of my subject? Am I straying beyond the proper field of my enquiry? Are my chosen boundaries still sensible and relevant and do I need to redefine the area of my research – would that be possible within the time that I have?
- What are my objectives? How do I justify working in this field and what are my more exact purposes? Have I explained my argument clearly? Are my objectives sensible given the field of activity I have defined for myself?
- What are my methods? Are they appropriate for the subject and the objectives of the research? Are they feasible methods in view of my time and resources?

Asking these questions at the beginning (when you may not yet have the answers) and constantly reminding yourself of them as the research progresses should enable you to demonstrate and judge the rigour of your research activity.

A careful and full consideration of these questions will also provide you with something else – when written down, these questions and answers should provide you with the best part of an introductory chapter to your thesis, in which you define the scope of your research and explain your objectives and methodology. You may find it very useful to sketch out such a chapter as soon as possible, firstly to provide you with a written checklist of what you are doing and why and how, but also to give you some confidence about writing up the research by feeling that you have actually made a start on that activity, so that it does not loom ahead of you in an intimidating way as the research progresses.

Putting your ideas in context

In defining and justifying your proposed research, you will also inevitably find yourself locating your project in the broader field of your subject. In explaining why your research is worthwhile, it will be necessary to point to gaps or unanswered questions in the existing body of learning and attempt to show how you intend to deal with this deficit. This part of the exercise should find expression in the part of your thesis which reports on the existing state of research and literature in the relevant field. This is likely to be an essential part of your argument, and it will also be of help to a reader of your thesis to have a summary of what work has been done so far and to cross-refer to details of this in a bibliography.

Working with your supervisor

Much of the designing and planning of research will be done in consultation with your supervisor, who may ask you specifically to address the questions above and to produce a draft outline of research activity. It is the role of the supervisor to help test your ideas as to the value and feasibility of your research subject and then to advise about appropriate approaches and methods. While this much is often appreciated very quickly by students, it may be less easy to determine more exactly how far the supervisor should go in this role of advice and assistance.

If at all in doubt on this issue, feel absolutely free to ask your supervisor for his or her own view of the role of supervision and what you may expect in that respect. The requirements of supervision may vary according to subject and discipline – in some subjects the student may be more easily left to his or her own devices in the library; in other areas the use of equipment or technology may require more detailed advice or supervision. Some institutions, or departments, may have written codes of practice or other notes of guidance that explain the mutual expectations of supervisor and student. If these are available ensure that you have a copy and that you are aware of what is laid down. This kind of documentation is helpful since it provides both students and supervisors with a clear idea of their respective roles and also gives the student something to 'wave' at the less than diligent supervisor. In the absence of such clear general guidance it is important to clarify with your supervisor the extent of the supervisory role and you should certainly not feel any reticence in doing so.

Subject to what may be specifically provided in institutional or departmental codes or notes of guidance or in degree regulations, there is a minimum level of advice that you may generally expect from your supervisor. You may reasonably expect your supervisor:

- to discuss your research ideas both with respect to the subject and method of your proposed research, with a view to being given the go-ahead for your project;
- to monitor your progress by responding to your own enquiries about how you should be proceeding with your research and by considering written reports or drafts of the thesis;
- to advise on the standard of the written thesis by considering a draft and to alert you as to any major omissions or defects in arguments.

It is never easy to draw a precise line as to the limit of the supervisor's role. Obviously, the supervisor must take care not to 'take over' the student's work and become, in effect, the author of the thesis. But on the other hand it would seem clear that the supervisor should guide the student around any major pitfalls. Your research effort should be independent but it is not expected that you can do absolutely everything for yourself.

Case studies

Adrian proves elusive

Adrian passed his examinations and other assessments comfortably, sometimes surprising the examiners with the depth of knowledge and degree of insight in his written answers. Shortly before taking a break after the examinations he called to see a potential supervisor for his thesis and briefly, but with a great deal of enthusiasm, outlined an idea for his research. This was sufficient to convince the lecturer that Adrian had identified a worthwhile and interesting topic to work on. Adrian then promised to submit a more detailed written proposal on his return from holiday two weeks later.

Four weeks later, Adrian's supervisor had neither seen nor heard anything from Adrian. The supervisor met him by chance outside the sports hall and asked if he had produced his draft thesis plan. Adrian explained that he had already completed the first part of his research and had accumulated 'a vast amount of material'. His supervisor expressed concern about the apparently unplanned nature of the research and insisted that they have a fuller discussion of objectives and methodology. An appointment was made for the following day.

Adrian failed to arrive for the meeting, but sent a note later that day explaining that he had been called away to an emergency meeting of the hockey club, but he also enclosed a detailed bibliography of the works he had consulted so far. Another meeting was arranged for two days later, at which Adrian did appear with a draft outline of his research. They discussed Adrian's proposal for an hour and a half, with a number of amendments being made at the supervisor's suggestion – Adrian's plan was overambitious for a Master's thesis. He admitted that a good deal of the work he had already done would have to be discarded, but cheerfully acknowledged that he now felt more confident about what he should be doing.

Nigel refuses to budge

Nigel was well ahead in his ideas for his thesis. After a seminar discussion earlier in the year he had approached the lecturer taking the seminar and said that he thought that one of the issues which had been debated raised some significant questions, which would serve as a good basis for a thesis. The lecturer agreed that there may be 'some mileage in the subject' and advised Nigel to contact him after the examinations to discuss the possibility further. Nigel felt convinced that the subject was ideal for his thesis and over the Easter break made a 5,000 word draft of the argument he wished to follow. He posted this to the lecturer, who replied that he had only had time to glance at the draft – however, it appeared to have some promise even though he also indicated some probable methodological problems. He suggested that they come back to the subject after the examination period.

Slightly resentful at what he felt was a rebuff, Nigel pursued his ideas further at weekends during the examination period. The day after his last examination he requested an interview with the lecturer, who he now called his supervisor, and insisted on presenting a defence of his proposed methodology. This led to a somewhat testy interchange with the lecturer/supervisor continuing to express doubts about Nigel's approach. Nigel became increasingly taciturn during this interview and left agreeing 'to give some thought' to the comments he had received.

Samantha agonises about her ability

The examination period had been very stressful for Samantha, although her results were consistently strong. But even before the examinations she had approached one of the professors in her department, explaining that she was starting to worry about the thesis and doubting whether she 'had the intellectual equipment for that sort of thing' and that she had a number of ideas although they were all 'probably rubbish'. The professor assured her that some of her ideas sounded extremely interesting and that he would be very pleased to discuss them further after the examinations. In the meantime he urged her to stop worrying about the thesis at this stage.

Samantha returned to discuss the thesis after the examinations and, after looking at three possible topics, the professor agreed to supervise one of the proposed subjects. Samantha again expressed doubt about her ability to complete the research – she said that she had never tried to write anything as long as 20,000 words and that she was capable of writing only short reports. She was also worried about stating the obvious and she was sure that there could not be much worthwhile in her research proposal because 'why else hasn't somebody already worked on this if it's that good?' Her supervisor patiently asked her to repeat her basic objectives and outline her area of research, which she did immediately with extreme clarity and concision. He said adamantly that he was quite happy with her proposal, but she left running her hand through her hair saying 'My god, I sometimes wonder why I ever started this!'

Discussion points

1. What skills do you think you will be able to develop in the process of carrying out research and writing up a thesis at Master's level?
2. Are you able to quantify the time available for the work to be done on your thesis? What allocation of time would you suggest for the main phases of activity required for producing the thesis?
3. Can you list the main questions which ought to be addressed in constructing an outline of a Master's research project? How would you incorporate these into a model outline or plan for a Master's thesis in your field?

Questions and answers

Q. I am unsure about the way in which the thesis fits into the overall scheme of study for the Master's degree and how to go about deciding on the subject matter of the thesis and arranging the supervision. How do I find out about this?

It may be that your university or department (or both) have documentation relating to your degree scheme, or of a more general nature, dealing with the structure of the course and the procedures for arranging supervision. Any detailed information in a code of practice or in degree scheme documentation could make all this clear to you. In the absence of sufficient guidance in this form you should approach the member of staff in your department who has responsibility for the degree programme – or your personal tutor, director of studies or mentor if you have been allocated to a member of staff for such individual guidance. If you are at all unsure about how the degree programme is organised or delivered, you should feel confident, at any stage during the course, about approaching appropriate staff in the department in order to resolve these uncertainties. Remember to check noticeboards, your mail box and/or email so as not to miss meetings. Check with secretarial staff if you are unsure which members of academic staff to approach.

Q. How do I know whether my ideas for research are sensible and realistic, and whether I am hitting the right level in my research work?

Both your proposal and research plans and the research activity itself should be discussed with your supervisor, and your supervisor should monitor your progress. Your department will not allow you to proceed with the research without supervision – in effect you will need your supervisor's approval of your plans and willingness to supervise the subject you have chosen. The process of supervision should also alert you to the appropriate standard of research activity and academic writing for purposes of a Master's thesis. If you are at risk of seriously going astray this should be evident to you from your supervisor's comments and your supervisor should be ready to offer constructive advice. At postgraduate level you are assumed to be capable of a fair measure of independent work, but you are not completely on your own – otherwise there would be no point in having any supervision.

Q. *I have been working for some time on my research but do not have a comfortable relationship with my supervisor. I am not sure whether this arises from a difference in temperament, or from problems in communication and understanding each other when we discuss my work, but the outcome is that I feel that my supervisor has a low opinion of me and this is undermining my confidence. What can I do about this?*

It is not always possible to achieve an ideal match between supervisor and student, either in terms of personality or even in the level of interest in and enthusiasm for the research subject. In practice something less than perfection may well have to be tolerated on both sides! Unfortunately in some cases a mismatch of personality, or other instances of disagreement, can lead to an irretrievably sour relationship which then threatens the viability of the thesis exercise. In such cases there should be departmental procedures in place for finding alternative supervision. Usually an approach should be made to either the degree programme coordinator, personal tutor or mentor (if allocated) or perhaps the head of department. If the department's documentation does not make it clear what to do in such cases then request a confidential meeting with any of the above persons. But consider the situation carefully and judge if it is little more than a problem of oversensitivity – both students and academics can be notoriously sensitive about criticisms of their work!

2 Understanding the Role of Theory

Colin Wight

One-minute overview

The aim in this chapter is to provide a brief introduction to theory and to explain its role in the research process. Whenever you do research you are already using theory, even if you don't know it. Scientists routinely use theoretical concepts all the time and generally have a clear idea of what makes a piece of research scientific, even if they have never explicitly thought about these issues. Out of the mass of available data, the researcher has to decide selectively on the most important factors, and theory guides this process. Researchers use theory differently in different types of research, but some type of theory is present in all research.

This chapter will help you to understand the key elements of theory and is structured under the following headings:
- the role of theory;
- key terms and the elements of theory;
- the main approaches to social theory;
- case studies;
- discussion points;
- questions and answers.

The role of theory

Suppose you were talking to a friend about racial conflict. Suppose also that you and your friend agree that people learn negative stereotypes about other racial groups from their friends and families. This seemingly casual discussion is using a very basic theory to understand a social phenomenon. As this example shows, people routinely use theories without making them explicit or labelling them as such. Politicians who claim that children who are raised by single mothers are more prone to crime are expressing a theory. Researchers engaged in the human genome project are using theories of DNA structure to guide their research.

Since all research involves some theory, the question is not *whether* you should use theory, but *how* you should use it. Having an understanding of theory makes it easier to read and understand someone else's research and to conduct your own. An awareness of the role of theory in the research process helps clarify murky issues. Being explicit about theory leads to better designed, easier to understand and better conducted studies.

Theories help us to make sense of interrelated phenomena and, in some instances, can help us to predict the outcomes that are likely to occur when certain conditions are met. Researchers who connect their work to theory can generate better ideas about what to look for in a study and develop conclusions with more implications for further research. Building and evaluating theory is, therefore, one of the most important objectives of science. Theory is also important because it is easy for researchers to lose sight of the larger picture when conducting research. It is easy to focus on accumulating data rather than on clarifying how the study fits into a more general understanding of the phenomena under study. So before, during, and after a piece of research, you need to continue to keep thinking theoretically.

Only naive researchers believe that theory is irrelevant to research or that a researcher just collects data. Researchers who attempt to proceed without theory or fail to make it explicit may waste time collecting useless data. They easily fall into the trap of vague and hazy thinking, faulty logic and develop and use imprecise concepts. Theory frames the way we look at and think about topics. It gives us concepts, provides basic assumptions, directs us to important questions and suggests ways for researchers to make sense of the data. But what is a theory? One common definition is:

> *a logically interrelated set of abstractions, ideas and propositions about empirical reality which organises knowledge about the world.*

For now this will suffice as a working definition, and would generally be accepted by most natural scientists. However, in the social sciences there is no real consensus on what theory is and we will consider alternatives later in this chapter. Until then, it will be useful to accept that theory:

- is present in all research;
- frames how we look at and think about a topic;
- helps to clarify how the study fits into a more general understanding of the phenomena under study;
- can generate better ideas about what to look for in a study and develop conclusions with more implications for further research;
- helps us to make sense of interrelated phenomena;
- leads to better designed, easier to understand and better conducted studies.

Key terms and the elements of theory

What do you think of when you hear the word "theory"? It sometimes seems to scare students, and often with good reasons. Theoretical language often seems incredibly obscure and abstract. The mental picture that many students have of theory is something that floats high among the clouds, a tangled web of jargon and abstractions that are irrelevant to the real world. Part of the problem here is simply unfamiliarity with the language and once the key terms are grasped there is no reason to treat theory as something only theorists do.

All theories possess some key elements and rest on a set of assumptions. The most important of these are the dreaded ...*ology* words – ontology, epistemology and methodology. Any word ending in 'ology' simply relates to a science or critical analysis of a subject. Hence we have physiology, geology, mineralogy, anthropology etc.

Ontology

The prefix 'ont' stems from the Greek word meaning 'to be' and ontology is the science of being or of existence. When philosophers talk of ontology they generally mean a systematic inquiry into the nature of existence itself. To a scientist, however, the term takes on a slightly different meaning. All theories have an ontology, or to put it simply they present an account of the phenomena under study and the relationships between these phenomena. This is the theory's ontology. The Watson–Crick theory of DNA structure, for example, claims that genes are made up of strands of material in the form of a double helix wound around one another about a common axis. This is an ontological claim about the nature of genetic material. Marx's theory of capitalist society suggests that there are dominant groups – the proletariat and the bourgeois – around which societal conflict occurs. This is a claim about the ontology of capitalist society. In this sense ontology simply refers to the assumptions about existence underlying any theory or piece of research. But there are different levels to a theory's ontology – the explicit and the implicit.

Concepts

Generally, a theory's ontology will be explicitly expressed in terms of concepts. These concepts are ideas expressed in terms of symbols or words. In many natural sciences these concepts are often presented in symbolic form – such as formulas or equations. Most social science concepts are expressed as words. Concepts are everywhere and we use them all the time, which only serves to illustrate that even in everyday life we theorise all of the time. The concepts we use in everyday life are often vague and unclear. Concepts used in research are much more rigorously defined and have very clear meanings. All theories require well-defined concepts.

Assumptions

As well as explicit and well-defined concepts, another part of a theory's ontology are the implicit assumptions. Most natural scientists tend to work on the assumption that reality, or the objects of inquiry, exist independent of theories about them. Some quantum scientists have challenged this assumption and philosophers regularly challenge it. Whether or not you think this a good assumption, the point is that it is an assumption that scientists rarely challenge. Think, for example, about the concept of a book – this assumes a system of writing, people who can read and the existence of paper. It is possible to do research into the use of reference books in libraries and never think about these deeper assumptions. One way for a researcher to deepen an understanding is to identify the assumptions on which the concepts are based.

Methodology

Methodology is the science or critical study of methods. You will often read textbooks on research methods that propose using a methodology. Strictly speaking this is incorrect – you use methods. Methodology is the systematic *assessment* or *study* of those methods. It is important that you think about the most appropriate methods given the theory's ontology. Hence ontology and methodology are inextricably linked. In a sense methodological questions follow naturally from ontology. It is no use, for example, attempting to interview atoms – unless, of course, it is part of your theory's ontology that atoms can talk!

Epistemology

Epistemology is often the most troubling of these '…ology' words, but it is actually quite a simple concept – although its implications are of major importance to researchers and, hence, it is often the subject of heated debate. As an 'ology' it is clearly a science of something, and that something is derived from the Greek word for knowledge, *episteme*. Epistemology is the science, or critical study, of knowledge. Typical epistemological issues are the definition of knowledge, the sources and criteria for knowledge claims, the kinds of knowledge possible, the validity of knowledge claims, and the relationship between the knowledge claim and the object of knowledge.

From this you should be able to see why it is so important an issue. Research makes knowledge claims and researchers should be prepared to spell out on what basis those claims are made. It is always a valid question to ask of a researcher, 'Which epistemology did you use?' This allows other researchers to evaluate the research results and, where possible, to check them using the same data and methods and the same epistemology. However, another equally valid question is whether or not the chosen epistemology was appropriate to the object under study.

It is often assumed that science uses experience and observation as the basis of knowledge claims, and while this is generally true it is not always the case. Mathematics, for example, does not observe or experience that $2 + 2 = 4$. We know that $2 + 2 = 4$ through a process of logical reasoning, not experience nor observation. Research that uses experience and observation is using an epistemology called *empiricism*. Research, such as mathematics, that uses logical reasoning is using an epistemology known as *rationalism*.

Although philosophers of science and social science spend much of their time debating the superiority of one epistemology over another, Einstein nicely spelled out the position adopted by most researchers – scientists have to be epistemological opportunists adopting the basis of knowledge claims to suit the object under study.

More often than not scientists will use more than one epistemology to substantiate their research findings. Take, for example, the way we experience a stick that appears to be bent in water. Our experience seems to tell us that the stick is bent in the water, and yet straight when out of water. But we know this is not the case and in this example we use rationalism – our faculties of reasoning – to make sense of what we experience. What this example also shows is the manner in which experience can deceive us. Because of examples like this, scientists generally take a sceptical stance on all knowledge claims and actively seek out many different forms of evidence using differing epistemologies.

The main approaches to social theory

Although the above discussion may have convinced you of the importance of theory to research, it has been based on a very one-dimensional view. This view may suffice for students in the natural sciences, but social science students need to be aware of some additional issues. Put simply, many social scientists argue that the ontology of the social world is so radically different from that of the natural world that a different view of theory is required.

Other social scientists take a different view and argue that it is possible to theorise about the social world in the same way that we theorise about the natural world, and that we can use the same methods to study both. However, whatever the differences between these approaches, theories in both the natural and social sciences will inevitably contain the elements discussed above.

Positivist social science

Positivism was a theory of science that gained prominence in the twentieth century. The term 'positivist' is generally used to relate to an approach to the social sciences that models itself on the natural sciences. However, students should be wary of this term since one can believe in the scientific study of society without accepting the positivist theory of science. Positivists base their account of science on an empiricist epistemology and tend to prefer quantitative data, often using experiments, surveys and statistics. They seek rigorous, exact measures and objective research, and they test hypotheses by analysing numbers carefully. Critics argue that positivism treats people as little more than numbers and that its concern with abstract laws and formulas are not relevant to the actual lives of real people.

Interpretative social science

Interpretative theorists argue that the positivist theory of science can not be applied to the social sciences because the objects of social science are so radically different. According to interpretative theorists, such as Max Weber, the social sciences need to study meaningful social action. This approach argues that simple observation will not enable us to distinguish a blink from a wink. Although the outward signs of blinking and winking are the same, winking differs from blinking in that it is intentional. Hence, these theorists argue that we must learn the personal reasons or motives that shape social behaviour. According to this approach, researchers conduct research to uncover the meanings embedded within social phenomena. When studying social events researchers need to get inside the social event in order to understand it. This is a radically different view of the relationship between the researcher and the object of inquiry from that of natural science.

Case studies

Jane puts theory into practice

Jane considers this all irrelevant. She is interested in studying subatomic particles and can see no benefit in theory. One way to see how theory helps to shape her research is to consider the nature of matter. Since the ancient Greeks we have had theories of matter, and had Jane been conducting her research then, it would have been very different – if indeed a woman would have been allowed to conduct research.

Ideas about matter have changed substantially since then, but some key moments stand out. The Becquerels' discovery of radioactivity in 1896, Planck's quantum theory formulated in 1901 and the acceptance of the general theory of relativity formulated by Einstein in 1916 have led to radical reformulation of the theory of atoms and classical physics. Among other things, scientists had to give up the ideas of:

- the atom as the smallest, indivisible unity of matter;
- the unchangeable material identity of atoms;
- the principle that it should be possible (in theory at least) to calculate and predict exactly the behaviour of single atoms.

- And Jane, at least insofar as she follows these dominant theories, will have given up these as well. So theories *are* shaping her research and an awareness of theory can be suggestive of further areas of research. For example, if atoms were the smallest indivisible unity of matter as we once thought then there would be little point in Jane looking for subatomic particles. Equally, Jane could attempt to challenge contemporary theories by trying to prove that these ideas should not have been discarded. So, for example, she could well attempt to show how it might be possible to predict the behaviour of single atoms exactly. To do this, however, she will still need a theory to guide her research – perhaps a theory she develops herself. In this way Nobel prizes beckon. .

Tom's research dilemma

Tom is interested in studying the role played by public opinion in shaping the attitude of government elites to poverty. He is worried about how he would go about researching such a topic and how he could ever prove his findings.

There are various theoretical options available to Tom. He could, for example, simply observe levels of public concern about poverty and relate this to the policy outputs of state agencies. The problem with this approach is that it would be very difficult to say that we really 'knew' (the question of epistemology) that it was public concern about poverty that was driving the policy outputs.

To get around this problem Tom might consider taking an interpretative approach to the issue and conducting interviews with policy makers to discover their attitudes, and whether these change in relation to public opinion. Equally, Tom is going to have to come up with theoretical accounts of public opinion, poverty and policy elites – and different theories will conceptualise these differently. Tom is going to have to be theoretically aware to ensure that he has coherent concepts of his entire cluster of variables and a clear theoretical understanding of how they relate to one another.

Catherine's lack of theory

Catherine is interested in the exploring the constitution of adult sexuality as determined by the interaction of genetic constitution *and* the environment. She is aware that one theory that attempts to explain just this is epigenetic theory (the study of mechanisms involved in the production of phenotypic complexity in morphogenesis). However, research using this theory is generally carried out in medical schools or as part of the biological sciences, and Catherine is interested in the 'social' mechanisms.

This is a difficult one. Social scientists tend to be very wary of any attempt to introduce a biological aspect as an explanation of social behaviour. Also, this type of research was discredited as a result of the practice of eugenics during World War II. There are clearly ethical and political issues raised in such research. However, since Catherine is interested in exploring the social mechanisms relating to adult sexuality, this shouldn't present too much of a problem.

The big problem is going to be finding a supervisor who knows enough about epigenetics in a social science department. Catherine's best bet is to find a research centre that can supply expertise in both fields. The transmission of theory from one field to another, however, is not easy – disciplines tend to have fairly clear ideas of the kinds of research they consider appropriate.

Discussion points

1. What kind of things are you interested in studying? How do they relate to other closely related phenomena? What aspect(s) of them do you wish to study?
2. What are the current competing theories in your field? What alternative avenues of research do they suggest?
3. How do theories come to dominate certain disciplines?

Questions and answers

Q. My supervisor is firmly committed to a particular theory, but I have my doubts. I value the opinion of my supervisor but

I want to challenge some of his research findings. What should I do?

This is often a worry for new students, but most supervisors like nothing better than to be challenged. From their perspective every attempt to falsify a theory can serve as an instance of confirmation. One famous philosopher of science – Karl Popper – even suggested that the attempt to falsify theories was what science is. If, however, your supervisor is totally unsupportive you may have to think about changing supervisors.

Q. *I have no idea how to set about studying my topic. Also, I don't want to spend loads of time ploughing through different theories. What can I do?*

First of all speak to your supervisor, other researchers and other students. You should be able to gauge which are the dominant theories at present. This doesn't mean that you have to follow them but it should narrow down the field. Alternatively, scan the latest textbooks to see what the current state of theoretical development is in your field. Go to conferences and talk to people – you'll soon get a feel for where the action is and what interests you and what doesn't.

Q. *I want to study voting behaviour, but there are so many theories and they all seem to make some sense. How do I go about comparing them?*

This is one of the most difficult of all questions. The short answer is that there are many differing theories about whether you can compare theories. These range from those that say that theories can be compared to those that say they can't – and, of course, all positions in between. This doesn't seem to help much does it? My advice is that if you want to compare theories you will need to ensure that you have a good theoretical defence of theory comparison in your thesis. However, don't fall into the trap of attempting to answer the question of whether theories *can* be compared – this isn't what you are interested in. Leave this difficult question to the philosophers of science – they need something to do.

Bibliography

Chalmers, A.F. (1992) *What is This Thing called Science?* Buckingham, Open University Press.

Delanty, G. (1997) *Social Science: Beyond Constructivism and Realism.* Buckingham, Open University Press.

Hammersley, M. (1997) *Social Research: Philosophy, Politics and Practice.* London, Sage.

Harré, R. (1970) *The Principles of Scientific Thinking.* London, Macmillan.

Kuhn, T. (1970) *The Structure of Scientific Revolutions.* Chicago, University of Chicago Press.

May, T. (1996) *Situating Social Theory.* Buckingham, Open University Press.

Popper, K. (1959) *The Logic of Scientific Discovery.* London, Hutchinson.

Sayer, A. (1992) *Method in Social Science: a Realist Approach.* London, Routledge.

Smith, M.J. (1998) *Social Science in Question.* London, Sage.

Constructing and Interpreting Qualitative Data

Mark Goodwin

One-minute overview

Depending on your subject area, your Master's thesis may well be based around an examination of qualitative data. This chapter will take you through the main methods used by researchers to construct and interpret such data.

In doing so it will cover the following areas:
- the nature and use of qualitative data;
- the construction of qualitative data;
- interpreting qualitative data;
- case studies;
- discussion points;
- questions and answers.

The nature and use of qualitative data

Qualitative data allow us to investigate people's beliefs, values and actions. They allow us to examine the meanings of social activities and enable us to situate these in a proper social context. They are non-numeric and may consist of words, pictures, sounds or symbols. They are used to investigate particular research problems – those where we want to understand how and why particular events and actions happen and where we want to know how people feel about such activities.

Qualitative data are often viewed as something separate to quantitative data, and the two are held to be quite distinct – requiring their own unique methods and approaches. Some students even have the idea that the two types should not be mixed, and feel they have to choose between one and the other. This is, however, somewhat misleading as both types of data will often be used in the same research project, and you may well need to use both in your own thesis. A project examining training schemes for the unemployed, for instance, may well use quantitative data to assess the level and extent of economic activity in a particular area, and then use qualitative data to investigate how people feel about the training schemes they have been on.

The misconception that the two types of data are utterly separate is strengthened by the belief that each has its own methods, and that once you have chosen which type of data you require then you are necessarily restricted in the methods you can use. This again is untrue – the same method can be used to generate both quantitative and qualitative data. You can use a questionnaire to ask people how often they go shopping (generating quantitative material) and you can also ask them what they feel about the experience (generating qualitative data). You can watch the way people behave in a meeting or in a classroom (qualitative data) and you can count the number of times they put their hands up (quantitative data).

The point is that the two types should not be seen as utterly separate. The key test here is appropriateness – you must choose a research method that will generate the type of research data you need, to answer the research questions that you have set. The research problem comes first, the type of data appropriate to it comes second, and the type of method you use to generate that data comes third. Always work from research question to data type to method.

Table 1 is taken from Andrew Sayer's book *Method in Social Science*. It is useful because it summarises how different types of research design ask different sorts of questions, define their research objectives differently and use different research techniques and methods.

Thus the difference between extensive and intensive research is not simply one of scale or breadth – it is one which affects all elements of the research process. Qualitative data will be more

	Intensive	Extensive
Research question	How does a process work in a particular case or small number of cases? What produces a certain change? What did the agents actually do?	What are the regularities, common patterns and distinguishing features of a population? How widely are certain characteristics or processes distributed or represented?
Relations	Substantial relations of connection.	Formal relations of similarity.
Type of groups studied	Causal groups.	Taxonomic groups.
Type of account produced	Causal explanation of the production of certain objects or events, though not necessarily representative ones.	Descriptive representative generalisations, lacking in explanatory penetration.
Typical methods	Study of individual agents in their causal contexts, interactive interviews, ethnography. Qualitative analysis.	Large-scale survey of population or representative sample, formal questionnaires, standardised interviews. Statistical analysis.
Limitations	Actual concrete patterns and contingent relations are unlikely to be 'representative', 'average' or generalisable. Necessary relations discovered will exist wherever their relata are present – e.g. causal powers of objects are generalisable to other contexts as they are necessary features of these objects.	Although representative of a whole population, they are unlikely to be generalisable to other populations at different times and places. Problem of ecological fallacy in making inferences about individuals. Limited explanatory power.
Appropriate tests	Corroboration.	Replication.

Source: Sayer (1992)

▲
**Table 1
Intensive and
extensive
research**

appropriate to addressing questions posed by intensive research where the aim is to understand the generation of particular processes and meanings in a small number of cases.

The construction of qualitative data

Because qualitative data deal with feelings, beliefs, values and emotions, they are largely unstructured. In other words, they are not sitting around neatly waiting to be collected by the researcher – they actually have to be constructed. Moreover, qualitative data are often constructed as part of a research process which directly involves other people as elements in that process – these data come from talking to people, from interviewing them, from watching and observing them or from discussing things with them in groups. Whatever method is used, the construction of qualitative data has to be seen as a social activity, not as a neutral or technical procedure. And because you will be dealing with other people in a social situation, the generation of qualitative data can be quite challenging and exciting. It can also be complex and difficult. It is not the easy option for those who simply wish to avoid encountering statistics – the methods that are employed to construct qualitative data have to be used in a rigorous and proper manner if those data are to be reliable and meaningful.

There is a range of different methods you can use to generate qualitative data – as mentioned before; the critical thing is to ensure that you decide on the ones which are appropriate for generating the type of data you need to address your particular research questions. Thus, no method is either right or wrong at the outset – they will simply be more or less appropriate for constructing data that are relevant to your particular thesis.

A more helpful distinction to draw than that between qualitative and quantitative data is perhaps that between data which you have to construct, as the researcher, and data which has already been constructed for you. Again your thesis will probably involve a mixture of the two. Table 2 gives you an idea of the range of sources and methods that can be used to generate each type of data.

Preconstructed data	Researcher-constructed data
Official data	Interviews
Academic reports/books	Participation and observation
Research reports	Questionnaires
Media output	Panels/focus groups

◀
Table 2
Sources of data

Essentially, all qualitative data can be constructed from one of three broad methods:

- Questioning (or talking to people) – the methods under this heading range from the standard questionnaire asked many times in the same format, to the one-off interview which is completely unstructured.
- Observation (or watching people) – these methods range from hidden observation to full participation.
- Documentary research (or reading) – again a range of methods is used drawing on material which is not just textual but involving any material which provides information to the researcher – for example videos, photographs, and paintings.

We will now look in more detail at each of these three broad ways of constructing qualitative data. It should be made clear that these are not mutually exclusive – just as a single piece of research might draw on quantitative and qualitative data, it may well generate its qualitative data from a variety of sources. The issue at stake here is not so much having to choose between one method or another, but using *all* those which are able to produce appropriate data. The key is to restrict the scale and scope of the research to that which can feasibly be conducted, given the timescale and resources available. Indeed, it is precisely because all students will be affected by such restrictions that a mixture of different methods might prove effective. Since we have our own restrictions, in that space is limited, we will give an initial flavour of each technique and provide a list of further reading at the end for those who wish to follow up and pursue particular methods in more detail.

Questioning and interviewing

This is perhaps the most common method of generating qualitative data. Indeed, if you think about it, talking to people is the most common way of gaining any information. The difference is that the techniques that are used inside research are rigorous and standardised. They range from the most structured formal questionnaire, where every respondent is asked the same question in the same order in the same way, to the unstructured informal interview, where the respondents themselves are left to guide the flow of conversation.

Questionnaires are often used to generate quantitative data but they can also act as a means of uncovering more qualitative information. Either way, they will be used to survey a relatively large number of respondents with very specific questions. Even where qualitative data are sought, these will often be analysed in a quantitative manner. You could, for instance, question the residents of a village about their attitudes to a new by-pass. You could ask them to grade their views about the by-pass from very necessary to totally unnecessary, and then quantify the results. In this way, attitudinal data, which is qualitative, can be analysed and presented in a quantitative manner. Indeed the purpose of a questionnaire is usually to undertake extensive research, seeking broad patterns of thought and behaviour within a sample population.

Other types of qualitative data do not lend themselves to quantification, since they concern the views and beliefs of individuals or of small groups. The purpose here is not to discover how many people share the same attitude (as with a questionnaire) but to uncover the meanings and intentions of specific actors in specific situations. In this instance, interviews will normally be used rather than questionnaires since the former offer a good means of examining experiences, feelings and values. You could, for instance, use interviews to find out why transport officials decided to build the by-pass around that particular village, or you could interview road protestors about why they were trying to prevent the by-pass from being built. In either case an interview would be an appropriate way of constructing the relevant data.

Interviews themselves, however, can vary in shape and form – again depending on what you need to know. As noted before, interviews are social activities involving other people and as such they have a social dynamic that has to be taken into account. They amount to far more than simply asking questions, and you need to be aware of the different ways in which questions can be asked and the different strategies that can be followed during an interview. Some interviews are much more like extended questionnaires, where a set pattern of questions are worked out beforehand and then asked in a precise order. This is known as a *structured open-ended* interview. The difference from a questionnaire is that the replies are not specified around particular sets of responses, but are open-ended – hence the name. In other instances the researcher begins the interview with a broad idea of the topics they wish to cover (this is called the *interview schedule*) but is prepared to let the drift of the conversation dictate both the order and content of the specific questions. This is known as a *semi-structured* interview.

In contrast to this, some interviews are almost completely unstructured – the researcher simply asks one or two questions at the beginning and then lets the interviewee structure the content and direction of the interview. This might be used, for instance, where you wish to uncover experiences and events which are significant to the respondent, but which cannot be foreseen in advance – or where you need to gain a life history or biographical account.

In some instances, interviews can be conducted with more than one person. Group interviews, or focus groups, are often used where the researcher is interested in the dynamics between the participants as well as in their individual responses. They can also be used in a situation where the responses of one person might encourage and stimulate responses from others. An example of each type of interview is given below – note that each is used to gain different kinds of information from different types of respondent.

The structured open-ended interview – for local residents

Preamble

I am interested in how you feel about the new by-pass and wish to ask you a series of questions about this. Your answers will be treated in the strictest confidence.

Questions

1. How does the by-pass affect you personally?
2. In what ways do you feel the by-pass might help or hinder the journeys you make?
3. How do you think the by-pass might affect the local environment?
4. Do you think the road might encourage more visitors to the area – if so which ones?
5. Do you think the council consulted you properly on the plans for the road?

The semi-structured interview – for members of a local residents' association

Preamble

I am interested in how your association feels about the new by-pass and wish to ask you a series of questions about this. I won't ask specific questions but I do wish to cover a number of topics. Your answers will be treated in the strictest confidence.

Topics to be covered

1. When did they join residents' association?
2. Did they join because of the by-pass?
3. What has been the attitude of the residents' association?
4. How successful have been the actions of the association?
5. Do you link up with other groups?
6. How has the local council responded to you?

The unstructured interview – for members of an environmental protest group

Preamble

I am interested in why you joined this group, and what you feel you can contribute to the environmental movement through your actions in opposing this road. Could you just tell me how you first got started in environmental protests?

Have you always had strong convictions against roads, for instance?

Topics to be covered

There is no predetermined agenda, and topics and questions simply arise from the flow of conversation.

The focus group – consisting of local councillors from one political party

Preamble

I am interested in how your party came to take the decision to go ahead with this by-pass. I'd like to ask you all a few questions – please feel free to chip in and contribute when you feel you can add to what's being said.

Topics to be covered

1. What were original political party views on the road?
2. What was the extent of any dissent?
3. How did they take views of local residents into account?
4. How important were the views of the planners?
5. Were the views of your party in London important?
6. How do you think the protestors will affect progress?

Participating and observing

Qualitative data can also be gained from watching people as well as talking to them. Again, this type of method varies depending on whether you are known to those you are observing, and on whether you are overt or covert in your research purpose. Possibilities range from complete participation to covert observation. In each case the object is for you, as the researcher, to be present and to watch as social events unfold around you. Your data comes from your own records and observations, not from the views of others. Hence the data comes from what people actually do (or your records of what they do) rather than from their recollections of what they did. Table 3 gives a summary of the different ways of gaining data through participating and observing. The precise method that is chosen will depend on the nature of the research subject and on the level of access available. Full participation will allow you to share the lifestyles and experiences of those under study.

	External observation	Participant observation
Overt	Researcher does not conceal their identity or purpose but does not participate in the group under study. E.g. observes protest actions at proposed by-pass from a vantage position at the side of the road.	Researcher does not conceal their identity or purpose and participates in the group under study. E.g. works for the local authority on a placement and observes road policy-making from within.
Covert	Researcher conceals their identity and purpose but does not join the group under study. E.g. observes protest actions at the proposed site by walking along public footpaths.	Researcher joins the group under study but does not tell them their purpose. E.g. joins the by-pass protest movement as a full member but does not reveal the research purpose.

Kitchen and Tate (2000) p. 220

Table 3
Collecting data through participating and observing

Just as interviewing amounts to far more than simply asking questions, observation amounts to far more than simply watching other people. Full participation involves the building of trust and acceptance. Overt observation involves the ability to record and to detail information in difficult situations. In either case you will be faced with a decision as to what to record and what to leave out – in other words you have to decide on the spot what is likely to be relevant and important data and what is not. Below are a number of useful tips for undertaking observational studies from Kitchen and Tate (2000) p. 224 (after Walcott (1995) pp. 96–101):

- Remember there is no such thing as just observing. A lens may have a centre and a periphery but it must be pointed somewhere.
- Review constantly what you are looking for, in terms of whether or not you are seeing it.
- Observation is necessarily an averaging out process and there will inevitably be times when you cannot sustain your attention.

- Try to assess what you are recording and why in terms of your research questions, rather than in terms of what appears obvious to the eye. What are you observing and why?
- Reflect critically on how you record the data in the field, and on your subsequent practices of writing that data up. Are you writing too much or too little?

Documents and texts

So far we have concentrated on data that is constructed by the researcher. By turning our attention to documents and texts as a source of qualitative data, we can now look at materials which have been constructed by others. As might be expected there is a vast range of data available from such sources. These might be in the form of written text, but might also include, for instance, electronic media, paintings, literature, photographs and architecture. The rule is not to restrict yourself to the most obvious documentary sources, but to use whichever 'texts' offer appropriate data for addressing your research questions. In addition to taking different forms, documentary sources have been constructed by others for all sorts of purposes. Those of potential interest to the researcher, as a source of qualitative data, might include personal documents such as diaries and letters, official documents such as minutes of local authority meetings or memos from a health authority, imaginative documents such as poems or paintings, and corporate documents such as company records and annual reports. There are a number of advantages in using documents for constructing qualitative data – Cloke et al. (2001) give the following:

- They can open up relatively inaccessible worlds. A famous study of Polish peasants migrating to the USA (Thomas and Znaniecki, 1927) was based on five groups of documentary data: letters to families and friends in Poland; a life history of one particular peasant; a collection of newspaper articles from Polish archives; a set of documents from social agencies in Poland and the USA; and a series of third person reports gleaned from social work agencies and court records.

- Documentary sources can also open up social worlds which, though accessible in principle, are actually relatively closed. Davis (1990) used a variety of newspaper reports, police documents and verbatim records of televised interviews to look at the military-style policing of contemporary Los Angeles, with particular reference to the so-called 'war on drugs'.
- Documentary sources offer the possibility of conducting historical and longitudinal studies, over a long time series.
- In a similar manner, just as they can be used to compare events across time, documentary sources can be used to analyse cross-cultural processes – comparing data from across a range of countries.
- Documentary materials are potentially very cheap and often easy to access. The researcher does not have to pay huge sums of money setting up research teams in a quest for material. The sources are often available in a record or reference library, and they are often collected together in a useable form.

What all documentary sources have in common is that they have been constructed for other purposes. Their primary purpose is not to provide research data, and thus it is important for the researcher to appreciate why and how they were initially constructed. As Hammersley and Atkinson (1984, p. 137) put it:

> *rather than being viewed as a (more or less biased) source of data ... documents ...should be treated as social products: they must be examined, not simply used as a resource. To treat them as a resource and not a topic is to ... treat as a reflection or document of the world phenomena that are actually produced by it.*

Thus we have to seek to establish the purpose behind the production of the document rather than just accept the record as somehow 'given'. Documents are not impartial and autonomous accounts of particular events and processes, instead they must be seen as integral to the institution, agency or individual that produced them.

There are a number of other potential difficulties involved in using documents. It is not a matter of simply pulling interesting-looking reports off a shelf and noting their contents. Scott (1990) sets out four key criteria involved in the use of documentary sources:

- Authenticity – is the source of the document correctly attributed?
- Credibility – is the source accurate and was it recorded with sincerity?
- Representativeness – is the source representative of opinion at that time and place? Are there alternative sources which might be used?
- Meaning – can the source be used in a literal sense, or is some level of interpretation required to understand the purposes of the recorder?

Sampling and selecting respondents

Whatever method of data construction is felt to be most appropriate, the researcher will have to carefully select those sources that can provide the most relevant information. To some extent this is fairly straightforward, as qualitative data is often used to explore purposeful activity or emotions in a limited number of cases. Thus, to understand how local residents feel about the construction of a by-pass, the researcher will need to approach those living near the proposed new road. However, even in this instance, limited time and resources may mean that the researcher can take only a sample of opinion rather than gathering from the whole population. A village of 500 homes will be too much for a Master's student to survey in its entirety, but a 10% sample of 50 respondents should be feasible. The issue arises as to which 50 – should they be selected at random or should they include certain numbers of specified groups to ensure a coverage of, say, elderly residents and new residents, or men and women, or car owners and non-car owners?

Things are rarely even this simple, and sometimes the researcher will have to spend considerable time identifying the most relevant respondents. Difficulties arise, for instance, when the focus of research is on the actions or decisions of an institution. Who inside that institution should be approached? If the research question is to account for the siting of the by-pass, rather than to analyse how local residents feel about it, this immediately raises additional questions. Who should be approached within the local authority that gave the go-ahead – the planners, the surveyors, the transport engineers? Should research concentrate on council officials or elected councillors? Should external agencies such as transport pressure groups or environmental activists be approached? How local should the research be, or will the researcher need to consult regional and national organisations?

These are all questions which arise at the outset of the research. Answering them goes hand-in-hand with choosing appropriate methods. Thought should be given to more than just how the research is to be undertaken – attention also needs to be paid to who the precise subjects of the research will be and especially to which individuals or groups – or sets of documents or collections of paintings – will provide the most relevant sources of data.

Interpreting qualitative data

As even this very brief overview will have shown, qualitative data comes in many guises. It is very rarely neat and ordered, and therefore a special importance must be placed on how such data is interpreted. In many ways, constructing and generating the data is only the beginning of the research process. An equally large task is analysing and making sense of the data. This is difficult, of course, because data never speak for themselves – they have to be interpreted by the researcher. When you return from fieldwork you will be faced with a collection of disparate and partial pieces of information – some relating to events, some to feelings, some given by individuals in an interview, some gathered from 50 respondents via a questionnaire. Your task is to pull all this together in a meaningful way so that your research questions can be investigated and answered.

Although it is difficult to be precise about the analysis of qualitative data because each research problem will generate different amounts and types of data, Dey (1993) has provided us with a very general scheme of interpretation. He maintains that all qualitative data will have to undergo three stages of analysis – they will have to be *described*, *classified* and then *connected*. Description simply involves the portrayal of data in a form that can be analysed – for qualitative data this is mainly textual. Thus, interviews will normally be recorded and the recording typed out as an interview transcript. This gives a verbatim record of what was said by all parties. Notes and records from observational fieldwork will usually be written up in the form of a research diary, detailing events in a temporal manner. Material from documents will usually have been recorded in note form, or may exist as complete photocopies, for instance.

To a certain extent, at this stage of the analysis the data will be in a fairly raw form. It thus needs organising and classifying. This is the point at which we enter the second stage of analysis. The jumble of data has to be put in order and sifted and sorted into meaningful sets. Thus, classification necessarily involves breaking your data up and moving it around. If you had transcripts of ten interviews with different local government officers all on the theme of the siting of the by-pass, you might wish to identify all the answers that mentioned the role of central government. These could then be extracted from the individual interviews, and placed alongside each other to gain an overall impression of what people considered to be the level of central involvement in the building of the road.

The third stage of data analysis involves connection. For Dey this involves more than just identifying similarities between different categories of data. It involves analysing the interconnections between different types of data. Dey uses a building analogy to clarify this. Whereas classification involves sorting all the bricks, windows, beams and frames into different piles, connection involves putting them together into a larger structure.

These three stages are not necessarily linear – there will be iterative procedures to be made at each stage, reflecting back on what has gone before and making modifications as a result. Figure 3 gives a representation of this process.

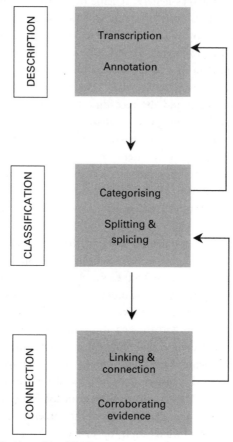

Kitchin and Tate (2000)

Fig. 3: Description, classification and connection of data

This whole procedure is necessarily complex. It is, for instance, more difficult to sift and sort qualitative data into workable categories than it is quantitative data, which do fall into ordinal, nominal, interval and ratio categories as the next chapter shows. The categories to be used for qualitative data are not so straightforward and have to be imposed by the researcher. The skill lies in being able to draw out the implications of different types of data, and connect them in a way which enables them to bear the weight of interpretation placed on them. In other words do not claim too much for your data, and only draw conclusions that you can substantiate. Your thesis will suffer if you try to claim too much which you cannot give evidence for – or indeed if you do not make enough of your material. The trick is to recognise that your conclusions will only be as good as the data you generate to support them.

Case studies

Glenda writes a letter

Glenda has planned her research project and knows that she wants to interview a range of local business people on their attitudes to the proposed local by-pass. However, she doesn't know how to go about this. The easiest way is to write letters asking for an interview – but who should she write to? Glenda remembers some important advice – that she should always identify an appropriate sampling frame from which to draw potential respondents. Since she hoped to interview people in business, Glenda decided to look through a commercial directory, or index, along with the *Yellow Pages* telephone directory. Having done this, she drew up a list of names and addresses of potential interviewees.

At the next stage, Glenda decided how many people she needed to interview in order to gather the necessary data. She then decided on a sampling strategy to select this number from her entire list. Once she had done this she sat down to write her letters, remembering that they should be short, informative and, above all, polite. Glenda needed to get 'in principle' permission to talk to those she had selected, but also realised that the details of the meeting could be fixed up and confirmed later, although she did feel it might be useful to suggest some dates in the letter, or even a broad timescale. She remembered to use headed paper and to give details of where she could be contacted if further details were required. She prepared herself for a few disappointments – after all, those chosen as potential respondents will rarely all say yes, and Glenda would need to work on a contingency plan in case some key respondents said no!

Terry forgets the tape recorder

Terry has gone to interview a local resident about the proposed new road. However, he is just about to begin the interview by asking if the interviewee minds being taped (consent is always vital) when he realises that he has forgotten to bring his tape recorder. For a moment he panics, wondering how he will record all the data. Then he remembers that he has a pencil and notepad, and he uses these to take down the main elements of what is said. He realises that he will not be able to use the data in quite the same way as if he had recorded it – he will not, for instance, be able to quote verbatim from the interview. However, he will be able to state broadly what the views of the respondent were.

On the way home he realises that this is a fairly common occurrence – he recalls other students telling him how they forgot to turn the tape on, or how they did not bring enough tapes. As soon as he gets home he sits down and writes up the main points raised in the interview. He vows to go through his checklist – tape recorder, tapes, interview schedule, batteries, notepad and pencil – more thoroughly next time.

Jane tries to interpret her data

Jane has worked hard to gather a range of data on the building of the proposed new by-pass. She has several interview transcripts, 100 questionnaire returns, notes of council meetings she attended as a member of the public, minutes taken from official meetings, and company reports from the firm that is building the road. She also has leaflets distributed by a protest group. Her problem is that some of these data sets seem to be telling a different story to others. In their report the road builders claim that they have local support, yet her questionnaire survey and the protest group leaflet claim local opposition. The person from the council's planning department told her he was responsible for the siting of the road, yet the surveyors claimed this responsibility.

She remembered that one way of resolving, and even accommodating, these types of differences is through a technique called triangulation. Jane checked each source against the others, looking for inconsistencies. She noticed, for instance, that later in the company report it mentioned that their survey showing support for the road was carried out on a county scale. Thus, the villagers and the protest group could legitimately claim a more local opposition. She also noted that in the official minutes of a council transport committee meeting the surveyors' department was thanked for its lead role in siting the road. Jane had been able to build up an account of the road's development which fully matched the evidence she presented. She was pleased that she had not claimed too much or too little from her data.

Discussion points

1. Can you think of alternative ways of constructing the data that you need to address your research questions?
2. How should you choose between the use of questionnaires and interviews, and between the use of different types of interviews?
3. Why are documents a useful source of qualitative data?

Questions and answers

Q. Can I mix qualitative and quantitative data in my thesis? I am worried because most text books treat these as completely separate.

You are perfectly entitled to mix quantitative and qualitative research. Indeed, in many projects this would be expected. The key point is that the two types of data are used to address different types of research questions – in this sense they are complementary rather than competing. You simply need to ensure that you are using the right data to address your research questions, and that you do not expect quantitative data dealing with broad regularities to answer questions about particular case studies that are better addressed through qualitative data.

Q. I have been told to do 50 questionnaires. Is this a good number?

How long is a piece of string? 50 may be a useful number and may generate the data you need, but it depends on the size of your total population. If you were undertaking research on schoolchildren and wanted to look at the behaviour of one class of 30, it would be possible to cover the entire population in 30 questionnaires. On the other hand if you were seeking to explore the attitudes of those living in a town of 5,000 to the closure of a local factory, then 50 may be too few. The general rule is to undertake as big a sample size as you can – within the obvious limits of time and other resources. We should insert here a real warning not to overstretch yourself. It also depends on how important the questionnaire data are to your overall study. If they are the key means of answering your research question then the more the better. If they are only one source amongst many then you may well have to limit the number in order to have the time to generate other types of data.

Q. *Should I record all my interviews? Will this make the interpretation of my data easier?*

It will and it won't! As a general rule, the clearer and cleaner the data then the easier the interpretation. This is why many researchers prefer to have all their data from interviews in a verbatim transcript. However, this is only absolutely necessary if you need to quote directly from the respondents. If you just want to gain a general impression of their views and attitudes then your notes of the interview will suffice. As a word of warning, it should be noted that interviews take a long time to transcribe and this should be built into your research timetable. As a rough guide, most researchers would allow one day of interpretation for every day spent constructing data.

Bibliography

Cloke, P., Crang, P., Goodwin, M., Painter, J. and Philo, C. (2002) *Practising Human Geography: The Construction and Interpretation of Geographical Data.* Sage.

Davis, M. (1990) *The City of Quartz.* Verso.

Dey, I. (1993) *Qualitative Data Analysis: A User Friendly Guide for Social Scientists.* Routledge.

Hammersley, M. and Atkinson, P. (1984) *Ethnograpy: Principles in Practice*. Routledge.

Kitchen, R. and Tate, N. (2000) *Conducting Research into Human Geography*. Prentice Hall.

Sayer, A. (1992) *Method in Social Science*. Routledge.

Scott, J. (1990) *A Matter of Record: Documentary Sources in Social Research*. Polity Press.

Thomas, W.I. and Znaniecki, F. (1927) *The Polish peasant in Europe and America* (2nd edition). New York: Dover (2 volumes).

Walcott, H. (1995) *The Art of Fieldwork*. AltaMira Press.

Additional helpful material

We have covered a wide range of issues in this chapter. The following list gives details of a variety of other books on qualitative data. Some concentrate on particular methods or specific forms of data, others are more general.

Berg, B. (1989) *Qualitative Research Methods for the Social Sciences*. Allyn and Bacon.

Burgess, R. (1984) *In the Field*. Allen and Unwin.

Frankfort-Nachmias, C. and Nachmias, D. (1996) *Research Methods in the Social Sciences*. Edward Arnold.

Mason, J. (1996) *Qualitative Researching*. Sage.

Rose, D. (1990) *Living the Ethnographic Life*. Sage.

Silverman, D. (1993) *Interpreting Qualitative Data: Methods for Analysing Talk, Text and Interaction*. Sage.

Strauss, A. (1987) *Qualitative Analysis for Social Scientists*. Cambridge University Press.

4 Analysing Quantitative Data

Alan Bond, John Brierley and Mark Tippett

One-minute overview

It may be that in the process of researching your Master's thesis, you generate some quantitative data that you need to analyse statistically so that you can see if you can be confident about what the data is telling you. This chapter cannot hope to explain what the appropriate statistical techniques are for your purposes – rather, the aim is to get you to think early on about your research design so that you produce data which *can* be analysed in a statistically meaningful way. There are some important measurement issues that you need to be aware of before embarking on empirical research, and some good advice can be given regarding research design with statistical analysis in mind.

This chapter will help you to start your research along the right lines with advice given under the following headings:
- explaining measurement rules;
- explaining measurement scales;
- designing research so that meaningful statistical operations can be applied;
- case studies;
- discussion points;
- questions and answers.

Explaining measurement rules

There are certain rules for measurement which were originally set out by Stevens (1946) in an article which is widely recognised in the social sciences as being of great value. You may think that work produced as long ago as 1946 has had sufficient time to become accepted, and its recommendations adopted in today's research. In fact, this is often not the case!

It is important that you become aware of the main features of Stevens' work so that you don't apply inappropriate statistical techniques to your data. If you do fall into this trap, you run the risk of reaching conclusions which, in reality, may have little or no supporting evidence. We need to start with a basic definition of the term 'measurement' – Stevens defined it as:

... the assignment of numerals to objects or events according to rules ...

So, for example, the metric system for the measurement of length uses a set of rules governed by an international organisation called the *General Conference on Weights and Measures*, and all the major countries of the world have a representative on this organisation. The rules are part of the *Système International* (SI), with which many will be familiar. It used to be that a measurement of one metre represented a standard length based on the length of a platinum–iridium alloy bar stored in France. The difficulty with a rule of measurement like this is that reproducibility is difficult in other countries because lengths have to be calibrated against this one bar. For this reason, the standard length was changed in 1960 to be equivalent to the wavelength of orange-red light emitted by atoms of krypton-86. Hence, one metre is now defined as 1,650,763.73 times the wavelength of this kind of light. This explanation is meant to illustrate that measurements can only take place according to rules which have been set – although in most cases you are probably completely unaware of the existence of such rules.

Measurement in its most general sense can be regarded as some form of *mapping* from a set of objects, events or properties onto some subset of the real numbers. Here there is a notation with which you need to be familiar in order to progress through this chapter. Take as an example the situation illustrated in Figure 4.

You have two sets of numbers. Each number in the first set, called the domain, is associated with just one number in the second set, called the range. This association is a function, or a mapping, and in this particular example is simply the square function. Therefore, each number in the domain of the function is mapped to an associated number in the range of the function.

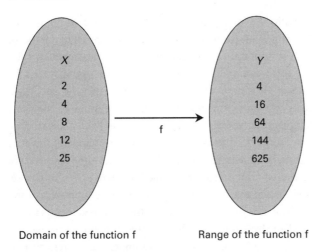

Domain of the function f   Range of the function f

Fig. 4: An example of a mapping

Now it is normal practice to collectively refer to the domain X, the range Y, and the functional relationship between them as a *measurement rule*. In other words, a measurement rule can be defined as:

A measurement rule has three components:

- a domain, X
- a range, Y
- and a mapping, f, from X into Y.

Figure 4 is a simple mathematical example of a measurement rule. A more familiar example is one in which a sequence of temperatures are recorded using the Centigrade rule. In this example, the measurement rule comprises a domain which contains the times at which the temperatures were taken, a range comprising the actual temperatures recorded at these times and a mapping from the domain to the range defined by the Centigrade rule. Another example involves the assessment of relative intelligence for a given set of individuals. Here intelligence is assessed by having individuals answer a standard set of questions with marks awarded to each question based on a rigidly defined marking rule. Hence, the measurement rule is comprised of a domain consisting of the set of individuals to which the test was applied, the range contains the intelligence scores they obtained according to a rule which awards marks based on a standard set of questions.

It is important to note, however, that measurement rules are often not unique – temperature, for example, can be measured using a variety of measurement rules and these rules will in general return different measures of the same temperature. For example, if we use the Fahrenheit rule we may come to the conclusion that the temperature at a particular time is 32 degrees. However, the same temperature measured on the Centigrade rule is 0 degrees. It is, of course, well known that once we have measured temperature using one rule it is easily converted to the 'equivalent' temperature implied by another rule. In the present example the relationship between temperature under the Fahrenheit rule (F) and the Centigrade rule (C) is given by the formula

$$F = C \times \frac{9}{5} + 32.$$

However, the fact that we can use different rules to measure the same phenomena has some very important implications for the types of statistical procedures we can apply to the data we end up using in our empirical work.

We can summarise the issues this raises in terms of three crucial 'identification' criteria. Before conducting empirical work, researchers should:

- identify the measurement rules (admissible measurement procedures) appropriate to the empirical situation being investigated;
- determine the group affiliation of the collection of measurement rules chosen;
- determine the 'statistical procedures' which may be *meaningfully* applied to the data they end up working with.

The importance of these identification issues can be demonstrated in terms of a simple numerical example. Imagine that we have two houses – A and B. We have taken measurements of the temperature in these two houses using the Centigrade rule, once at 8 o'clock in the morning, and once at 5 o'clock in the afternoon, on the same day. Table 4 sets out the results.

House	Temperature at 8 a.m.	Temperature at 5 p.m.
A	2°C	10°C
B	4°C	6°C

◄
Table 4:
House
temperatures in
degrees
Centigrade

We could also have taken measurements in Fahrenheit, or we could simply convert the temperatures to the Fahrenheit measurement rule using the standard formula given above – these are given in Table 5.

Suppose you wanted to know if house A is hotter than house B. One thing you could do is calculate the geometric means of the pairs of temperatures for each house. This is calculated by multiplying the two temperature measurements and taking the square root of the result $\left(\sqrt{T_1 \times T_2}\right)$. Table 6 sets out the results of these calculations.

You can see that this method of comparison gives conflicting results. It thus follows that the geometric mean is

House	Temperature at 8 a.m.	Temperature at 5 p.m.
A	35.6°F	50.0°F
B	39.2°F	42.8°F

◄
Table 5:
House
temperatures in
degrees
Fahrenheit

House	Temperature at 8 a.m.	Temperature at 5 p.m.	Geometric mean	Deduction
A	2°C	10°C	4.47°C	House B is hotter than house A
B	4°C	6°C	4.90°C	
A	35.6°F	50.0°F	42.19°F	House A is hotter than house B
B	39.2°F	42.8°F	40.96°F	

▲
Table 6:
Geometric means
of the house
temperatures

a meaningless statistic if applied to a temperature series. It goes without saying that those interested in scholarly research would prefer to avoid problems like this!

Explaining measurement scales

Having exemplified the kinds of problems that can be encountered in quantitative analysis, this section goes on to identify statistical operations that can be applied to data meaningfully. It should be emphasised that it is beyond the scope of this chapter to provide instructions on the statistical tools themselves. The aim is simply to identify *appropriate* statistical operations that can be applied to different measurement rules. Armed with this knowledge you will be in a position to design research accordingly, and you will be able to seek advice more quickly regarding the application of the statistical tools you want to use.

The first thing you need to know is the measurement rule you are dealing with – there is a definition which can help:

The measurement rules f and g are J-scaled if there exists a function, π, in J such that $g = \pi \times f$. A measurement scale C_J is a collection of measurement rules which are mutually J scaled.

This definition is rather technical so an example will be given to explain what it means. In the measurement of temperature we can move between the Centigrade (C) and Fahrenheit (F) measurement rules by applying the transformation $F = C \times \frac{9}{5} + 32$ appropriately. This transformation is a member of the general linear group and so it follows from the above definition that the Centigrade and Fahrenheit measurement rules are members of the scale defined by this group. However, note that while there is a linear relationship between temperatures based on the Centigrade rule and temperatures based on the Fahrenheit rule, the temperature at which water freezes is different under the two rules. On the centigrade rule water freezes at a temperature of 0°C, while on the Fahrenheit rule it freezes at 32°F. In other words, the 'zero point', the temperature at which water freezes, is arbitrarily determined. Hence, Stevens (1946) suggested that instead of saying that temperature is defined on the general linear group scale, which is a bit of a mouthful, we say instead that it is defined on the 'interval scale'. This is because the difference (or interval) between two temperatures does have a natural zero point.

We can demonstrate this by considering the maximum and minimum temperatures on a given day which, for example, might be 14°C and 4°C respectively based on the Centigrade rule. It follows that the difference between the maximum and minimum temperatures is 10°C. However, under the Fahrenheit rule the maximum temperature is 57.2°F and the minimum 39.2°F. Therefore, the difference is $57.2 - 39.2 = 18.0$°F. But this could just as easily have been calculated by using the transformation rule, $F = 10 \times \dfrac{9}{5} = 18$. It follows that if the difference (or interval) between two temperatures based on the Centigrade rule is zero, then the difference between the two temperatures will also be zero if the Fahrenheit rule is used.

Stevens also suggested that there are three other measurement scales which are likely to be useful when handling data. These, along with the interval scale are displayed in Table 7.

Scale	Basic operations	Group structure (J)
Nominal	Determination of equality	Permutation group (any one-to-one substitution)
Ordinal	Determination of greater or less than	Order preserving group (any monotonic increasing function)
Interval	Determination of equality of intervals or differences	General linear group, $y = a + bx$
Ratio	Determination of equality of ratios	Similarity group, $y = bx$

▲
Table 7:
Stevens' scales
of measurement

Note that each of these scales is defined by the group affiliation of the transformations which define the relationship between its measurement rules. Thus, in Stevens' scheme, measurement occurs on a nominal, ordinal, interval or ratio scale according to whether each pair of admissible measurement rules involves determination of equality (the permutation group), determination of greater or less than (isotonic group), determination of equality of intervals or differences (general linear group), and the determination of equality of ratios (similarity group).

Table 7 is important because it categorises data into one of four scales. The next section will develop this further and will demonstrate how these scales can be used to determine whether particular statistical techniques are valid or not.

Designing research so that meaningful statistical operations can be applied

Taken by themselves, the measurement scales are a convenient device for classifying data according to the transformations which may be legitimately applied to them. While this is important, their most important role is in determining the 'statistical procedures' which can meaningfully be applied to data defined in terms of a particular scale. This 'statistical meaningfulness' concept, which was in fact demonstrated in terms of the temperature data above, is defined mathematically as follows:

> A 'numerical procedure' Φ is said to be $J(\sim, f)$ scale meaningful if, when $\Phi(f') \sim \Phi(f'')$, $\Phi(\pi \times f') \sim \Phi(\pi \times f'')$ for all f', f'' in C_J and π in J.

The previous definition of a measurement scale told us that the J measurement scale C_J is a collection of measurement rules which are mutually J-scaled. This definition develops this and gives a technical specification by which we can work out when a statistical procedure can be correctly applied to data. In this new definition, the tilde ($\sim$) simply represents one of the arithmetic operations 'greater than' ($>$), 'equivalence' (=) or combinations thereof (≤ or ≥). The definition requires that if a particular relationship holds between two sets of data then it should also hold if the data are transformed in a legitimate way – by using an alternative measurement rule. In the temperature example referred to earlier, it was shown that the relationship between two geometric means can be changed (reversed) simply by restating data from the Centigrade to the Fahrenheit rule. It thus follows that the relationship required for a statistic to be meaningful is violated and so we conclude that the geometric mean is a *meaningless* statistic if applied to data defined in terms of the interval scale.

The potential for problems of this kind are much greater in the social sciences where it can often be difficult, or even impossible, to define a unique unit of measurement. We can illustrate this by considering two sets of hypothetical data of IQ scores (measuring intelligence). In this example we consider two classes, A and B. Table 8 presents the results of the IQ tests taken by the three hypothetical students in each class.

The average intelligence score for class A is 98 while that for class B is 100. Hence, we might be tempted to think that 'on average' members of class A are less intelligent than members of class B. However, as with many intelligence assessment procedures, the unit of measurement is somewhat arbitrary, and here a higher score merely indicates that there is a higher level of intelligence – it says nothing about relative differences in intelligence. Hence, any order preserving (or isotonic) transformation may be applied to the data – and

	Class A	Class B
Student 1	60	50
Student 2	94	100
Student 3	140	150
Average	$\dfrac{60 + 94 + 140}{3} = 98$	$\dfrac{50 + 100 + 150}{3} = 100$

◄ Table 8: Intelligence scores in two hypothetical classes

	Class A	Class B
Student 1	$\log_{10}(60)$ = 1.778	$\log_{10}(50)$ = 1.699
Student 2	$\log_{10}(94)$ = 1.973	$\log_{10}(100)$ = 2.000
Student 3	$\log_{10}(140)$ = 2.146	$\log_{10}(150)$ = 2.176
Average	1.966	1.958

Table 7 identifies the data as being defined on the ordinal scale.

If, for example, we transform the data by taking the common logarithm of the 'raw' intelligence scores, we get a new set of intelligence measures as shown in Table 9.

Now we have the result that the average for the transformed data for class A is 1.966 while that for class B is 1.958. Hence, while the 'raw' data lead us to conclude that, on average, class B is more intelligent than class A, the transformed data lead us to exactly the opposite conclusion. This means that the average is a meaningless statistic if applied to data defined on the ordinal scale.

A summary of the meaningful statistical operations which can be applied to data defined on Stevens' four scales is detailed in Table 10.

Hence, suppose we have two sets of data, A and B, and that our calculations indicate that the variance (square of the standard deviation) of the group A data exceeds the variance of the group B data. If we transform both sets of data by a function from the general linear group, then Table 10 shows that the variance of the transformed data for group A will still exceed the variance of the transformed data for group B. Similarly, if the average for the group A data exceeds the average for the group B data, then Table 10 shows that the average of the transformed group A data will exceed the average of the group B transformed data. In other words, both the average and the variance are *meaningful* statistics if applied to data defined on the interval scale. Furthermore, since the similarity group (of the ratio scale) is a special case of the general linear group (of the interval scale) in that it uses

Scale	Basic operations	Group structure (J)	Meaningful statistics
Nominal	Determination of equality	Permutation group (any one-to-one substitution	Number of cases Mode Contingency correlation
Ordinal	Determination of greater or less than	Order preserving group (any monotonic) increasing function)	Median Percentiles Rank order correlation
Interval	Determination of equality of intervals or differences	General linear group, $y = a + bx$	Average Variance Product moment correlation
Ratio	Determination of equality of ratios	Similarity group, $y = b x$	Geometric mean Coefficient of variation Ratios of two measurements

▲
Table 10: Stevens' scales of measurement (Table 7) extended to the application of meaningful statistics

linear transformations with a unique zero (a is set equal to zero in the group structure which defines the ratio scale) then both the average and variance will also be meaningful statistics on the ratio scale. However, as the intelligence score example in Tables 8 and 9 and the accompanying discussion shows, neither the average nor the variance will be meaningful statistics for data defined on the ordinal or nominal scales. Similarly, while the median is a meaningful statistic for data defined on the ordinal scale, it is also a meaningful statistic for data defined on the interval and ratio scales. It is not, however, a meaningful statistic for data defined on the nominal scale. In other words, the 'meaningful statistics' column of Table 10 is cumulative. Hence, while the mode is a meaningful statistic for data defined on the ratio scale, neither the geometric mean nor the coefficient of variation are meaningful statistics for data defined on the nominal, ordinal or interval scales.

Case studies

Freddy and the average student

Freddy is a conscientious lecturer who thinks carefully about the grades he allocates to the students in his charge. He has two tutorial classes in his hamburgerology course – the first is predominantly made up of extremely bright students, although there are a few not so bright students as well, while the second is composed only of 'average' students. In the most recent examination set by Freddy the first tutorial group returned a much higher average mark than the second and, as Freddy expected, the dispersion of marks as measured by the standard deviation was higher for the first compared to the second.

Unfortunately, Freddy had made the mistake of setting an examination which was far too difficult and the university authorities asked him to 'scale' the examination marks so that a higher proportion of students obtained a mark in excess of 50%. Freddy did so but now finds that the first tutorial group returns both an average mark and a standard deviation of marks lower than those for the second group. Freddy is perplexed by this until the university's Registrar points out that his students' examination marks are defined on the ordinal scale. Since neither the average nor the standard deviation are meaningful statistics when applied to such data defined on the ordinal scale, it is not surprising that Freddy should find that results obtained using one measurement rule are 'reversed' when he uses an alternative rule.

Linda finds the difference

Linda is writing a thesis about the differences between male and female employees in a multinational company. She has obtained information about their level of educational achievement – which she defines as leaving full-time education after completing UK GCSEs, A-levels, first degree, Master's degree and a PhD – and codes these as 1, 2, 3, 4 and 5 respectively. Linda tested the difference in the educational achievement between male and female employees using a t-test. Her supervisor pointed out that the t-test can be applied only to data measured on an interval or ratio scale, and that the educational achievement variable is measured on an ordinal scale. The supervisor pointed out that the appropriate test for assessing the difference between the educational achievement of males and females is the Mann-Whitney test.

James learns from his mistake

James was analysing data concerning officer rank and tenure in months of a group of soldiers. He gave the analysis to his supervisor to review. The supervisor found that James had assessed the relationship between rank and tenure by calculating the product moment correlation coefficient between them. The supervisor recognised that this is an inappropriate statistical test because the product moment correlation coefficient can be applied only to data measured on an interval or ratio scale. The soldiers' rank is ordinal scaled data and the appropriate test to apply is the Spearman's Rank correlation coefficient. When James' supervisor told James that the statistical analysis was incorrect James was disappointed, but determined to carry out the statistical analysis again correctly.

Discussion points

1. Why is it important to ensure that appropriate statistical tests are applied to data?
2. Which statistical tests are the most appropriate for analysing nominal, ordinal, interval and ratio scaled data?
3. What are the implications of applying an inappropriate statistical test to nominal, ordinal, interval and ratio scaled data?

Questions and answers

Q. *I have obtained information about the grades of students in a test. The grades are 5, 4, 3, 2 and 1 – with 5 representing the highest grade and 1 representing the lowest grade. Which statistical tests can I apply to this data?*

This is ordinal scaled data because the grades assigned to the test results indicate that there is a relationship between the grades. Namely, 5 is a higher grade than 4, 3, 2 or 1, 4 is a higher grade than 3, 2, or 1 etc. – but there is no indication of the size of the interval between grades. The only statistical tests that may be applied to this data are those appropriate for nominal and ordinal scaled data. These include the mode and median. The mean cannot be used because this statistical test is permissible only when there is at least interval scaled data.

Q. *I have been given some data about the country of origin of students. How should I analyse it?*

These data are recorded on a nominal measurement scale. This scale is used to classify objects into particular categories. In this case students are classified into their country of origin. The coding used to classify the various countries may be changed without altering the basic information provided. The only permissible statistical tests are those which are unaffected by any changes in the coding of data, such as the mode and frequency counts.

Q. *I want to assess the correlation between the height in centimetres and weight in kilograms of a group of students. What is the most appropriate statistical test?*

As both height and weight are measured using a ratio scale, the most appropriate statistical test for assessing the correlation between them is the product moment correlation. This should be used in preference to the rank order correlation, which is a less powerful statistical test that should be applied when at least one of the scales of measurement is an ordinal scale.

Bibliography

Stevens, S. (1946) 'On the Theory of the Scales of Measurement' in *Science*, CIII (7 June) pp. 677–680.

Additional helpful material

Campbell, N. (1952) *What is Science?* Dover Publications.

Cohen, J. and Chen, P. (1983) *Applied Multiple Regression/ Correlation Analysis for the Behavioral Sciences*. New Jersey, Lawrence Erlbaum Associates.

Conover, W. (1980) *Practical Non-parametric Statistics.* New York, John Wiley.

Giles, J. (1972) *Real Analysis.* Sydney, John Wiley.

Shock, N. (1951) 'Growth Curves' in *Handbook of Experimental Psychology*, S. Stevens (Ed.). New York, John Wiley & Sons, pp. 330–346.

Siegel, S. and Castellan, N. (1988) *Non-parametric Statistics for the Behavioral Sciences.* New York, McGraw-Hill.

Stevens, S. (1951) *Handbook of Experimental Psychology.* New York, John Wiley.

Stevens, S. (1955) 'On the Averaging of Data' in *Science*, CXXI (28 January), pp. 113–116.

Stevens, S. (1968) 'Measurement, Statistics and the Schemapiric View' in *Science*, CLXI (30 August) pp. 849–856.

Torgerson, W. (1958) *Theory and Methods of Scaling.* New York, John Wiley.

5

Getting Down to Brass Tacks: The Hard Graft of Writing

Norma Green

One-minute overview

The deadline is looming but it is not easy to commit thought and findings to hard copy. Overcoming the writer's block and producing a product of which you can be rightly proud takes time and effort. However, there are steps and processes which can ease the pain and smooth the rough places.

In this chapter you will find help under the following headings:

■ preparing for writing;

■ mobilising parallel skills;

■ engaging in the writing process;

■ adjusting the nuts and bolts;

■ case studies;

■ discussion points;

■ questions and answers.

Preparing for writing

Writing is more than a mechanical process. It is not only a revelation of what you have learnt, discovered or worked out, it is also a statement of your beliefs and, by your style, a portrayal of yourself. The commitment of ideas to the written word requires determination. There are two requirements when preparing to write:

● mental readiness;

● the physical necessities.

How can I be mentally ready to write?

A lot of reading and thinking to clarify your purpose and goals needs to precede writing. You have been immersed in the detail of your subject. You need to step back and survey from a distance what you have gleaned, with a critical eye for prioritisation. You must convey concisely and accurately what you consider to be the kernels of your investigation. You may have written your thesis statement a long time ago. Perhaps it needs adjusting now. Your attitude needs to be positive and your confidence firm.

You may have a procrastinating nature. Allow yourself the activities of procrastination and you will probably speed your passage through it toward being able to get started. You need to be *ready* to write, so unfinished business, pressing priorities and personal rituals all need to be dealt with to clear your mind to face the task of writing. Fear of the commitment required by the writing process feeds procrastination. You need to take courage. Your writing will be more satisfactory if you make this necessary mental journey.

Hall (1994) identified three stages of writer's block – any one of which may occur during the writing process. You may find you cannot begin *to work at all*, or you may be unable to begin *to write*, or you may be unable *to finish* what you have begun. The key to solving these difficulties is to identify them and then to deal with the root problem.

What do I need to do to be physically prepared?

It is easy to overlook the importance of the obvious requirements, but if you don't make provision you will find the writing process more tedious and less inspired. You need to:

- identify your time(s) of day for optimum production;
- organise your references, notes and necessary equipment for writing;
- provide space, light, a comfortable temperature and coffee;
- choose a comfortable place (or places) to work where you feel productive and won't be distracted.

Most people have an optimum time for productive work. If you are not a morning person, don't force yourself into the early-bird mode. Work regularly at your best times. Take breaks. Eat regularly and take exercise. Establish and maintain a routine.

Choose a comfortable, convenient place to work – or, if you thrive on variety, have more than one place – where the conditions are conducive to productive work. Organise yourself so that everything you need is to hand. Keep it together. Tidy up after each session. Write yourself a note about what you want to do next so that when you start again, you don't start cold.

Mobilising parallel skills

The success of the finished thesis depends not only on the ability of the researcher to undertake research and to write clearly, but also on the skills involving:

- searching
- reading
- note-taking
- record keeping.

Searching for relevant material

Beginning a search does not need to be random or aimless. Begin with the bibliography of the definitive text – use reading lists produced by your supervisor or lecturers, or leads from discussions with colleagues. It is essential to be efficient in the use of search tools – OPACS *Libertas* binary word search of your own library catalogue, or JANET in other academic libraries and/or databases (such as BIDS/ISI and OCLC FirstSearch). Since the Internet carries so much up-to-date information, you should bookmark sites and download documents in order to make the best use of your time. Web search engines are also invaluable.

Reading actively and critically

In order to discover the context of your research, active critical reading must take place. Employing an appropriate speed of reading develops your strategy of attack on the volume of

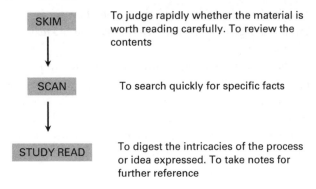

Fig. 5: Active and critical reading strategies

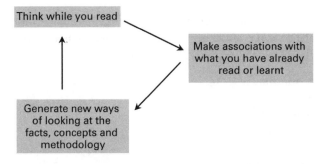

Fig. 6: How to read actively

material you have to handle. You may *skim*, *scan* or *study read* as shown in Figure 5.

Whatever strategy you employ, the most effective way to read is *actively*. Figure 6 sets out the process you need to follow to do this.

It is also essential that you read critically, as shown in Figure 7.

Record keeping to save valuable time

The one activity that can wreck your timetable is the preparation of a bibliography. You can be chasing elusive references you are sure you read somewhere ages ago to get complete bibliographic data – unless you resolve to keep a record of every source (book, article, unpublished paper, website) you ever opened from the very beginning of your work. You save valuable time and endless frustration by

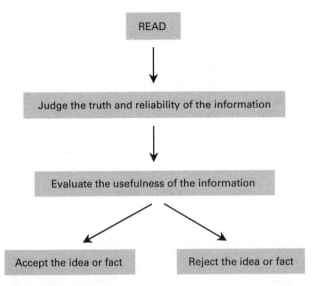

Fig. 7: How to read critically

recording all the essentials in a consistent format as soon as you access any source. Make value judgements of the contents. If the reference is useless to you, or appears that way when you first look at it, you should make a note to that effect so that you don't waste time in double handling. Noting the date when you first found the source is useful, especially when accessing websites. A note detailing the scope of the reference is also helpful. If you alphabetise your sources, you are well on the way towards finalising your bibliography. Figures 8 and 9 suggest formats you may find useful.

Plagiarism is academic theft. Read your university regulations on plagiarism to be very clear about how exactly you need to acknowledge someone else's work. Put the author's name, an identifying title and the actual page number where you keep your notes of sources read, and you will be unlikely to fail to acknowledge your sources.

Engaging in the writing process

Some supervisors ask candidates to prepare a literature review following reading around a subject. Others may ask for background information which will form at least part of the

```
Author's surname........... First name .............. Editor? ....
Topic ......................................................
Book title .................................................... Edition ..........
Place of publication ................. Date of publication ..........
Publisher ...................... Pages ......... ISBN....................
Date seen ........... Source ...............................
Comment on scope and usefulness ...............................
.............................................................................
.............................................................................
.............................................................................
```

Fig. 8: Sample bibliographic card entry for a book

```
Author's surname....................... First name ...................
Topic .........................................................................
Paper title .................................................................
Journal ....................................... Volume ...... Issue .......
Date of publication ........... Pages ......... Date seen ..........
Comment on scope and usefulness ...............................
.............................................................................
.............................................................................
.............................................................................
```

Fig. 9: Sample bibliographic card entry for a journal

introduction to the thesis. Others may suggest that you begin writing up your 'materials' and 'methods' sections first. Whenever you begin writing, you need to gather your thoughts before you actually start. The writing process, which is summarised in Figure 10, includes:

- brainstorming
- prioritising and planning
- drafting
- observing academic writing conventions
- redrafting.

Brainstorming and organising ideas

Brainstorming should follow reading, which provides the grist for the exercise. Trite as it may sound, a session of allowing

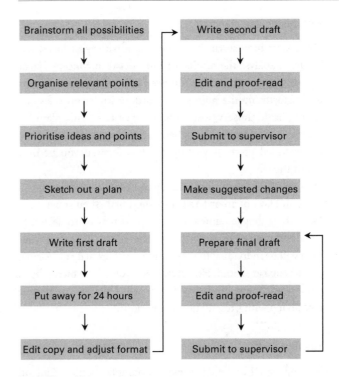

```
Brainstorm all possibilities  ─►  Write second draft
           │                              │
           ▼                              ▼
Organise relevant points         Edit and proof-read
           │                              │
           ▼                              ▼
Prioritise ideas and points       Submit to supervisor
           │                              │
           ▼                              ▼
   Sketch out a plan             Make suggested changes
           │                              │
           ▼                              ▼
   Write first draft               Prepare final draft  ◄─┐
           │                              │               │
           ▼                              ▼               │
Put away for 24 hours             Edit and proof-read     │
           │                              │               │
           ▼                              ▼               │
Edit copy and adjust format ─┘     Submit to supervisor ──┘
```

Fig. 10: The writing process

your mind the freedom of ranging unleashed around the concepts of your topic will produce a large share of the central considerations, relationships and interrelationships around which to build your thesis. Set yourself a time limit in a quiet place and write notes at random without making any judgement of anything you are writing.

Once these points are committed to paper, the process of evaluating their relevance and ordering them can begin. However, you may prefer to draw a mind map (Buzan, 1988) or produce a spidergram in your brainstorming session rather than work out the relationships after brainstorming. If so, you might like to use the *Inspiration* program which provides a way of mind mapping on screen. The important point is to engage in *unfettered thought* to draw out the essential elements of the topic and also to envision new relationships among the concepts. You then have plenty of material to draw from when you 'dry up'.

Prioritising and planning

Once your brainstorm has produced a battery of ideas, you ought to analyse the results for links between concepts, facts, elements, facets and ideas. You need to be ruthless in selecting and prioritising the points – discarding irrelevant ones and setting aside those whose value is uncertain. This planning stage is central to your work because the longer you labour on an extended piece of writing the less focused you become about the whole.

If you have taken time initially to isolate all the significant ideas and lay out an ordered consistent plan, then you are less likely to get bogged down in details that may be irrelevant to the development of your thesis. The actual format of your plan will be individual to you – and not necessarily the format you learned at school! However, if you follow the hierarchy of your department house style, you will have an easier time complying with presentation regulations.

The first draft

Writing is a building process. Paragraph should build on paragraph – expanding, exploring and arguing the case. Ideas should follow a clear sequence to take the reader with you. The first paragraph should be in the present tense to establish the scope, to suggest the parameters and their limits and to introduce definitions relevant to the thesis. A microcosm of the paragraph is given in Figure 11 – you can use this as a template for your own writing.

Observing academic writing conventions

Paying careful attention to your writing style helps the reader's understanding of your point of view, the details of your research, your analysis and your conclusions. You should aim for:

- cohesion
- clarity
- conciseness
- impersonal style
- consistency.

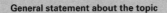

General statement about the topic

Focus on the important distinguishing characteristics you
want to emphasise

Probably in one sentence

↓

Expansion of the main points

Write something about each part of the general statement using the
same order you used above

Perhaps two or three sentences

↓

Examples of aspects of the topic

Choose one or more of these:
- quotations – properly cited
- examples of important aspects
- examples of unusual aspects which strengthen your point of view

Possibly up to five sentences

↓

Summary and concluding statement

Draw together the main ideas by briefly mentioning each and
suggesting where you have reached at this point. You could include
something that provides a bridge to the next aspect

Probably in two or three sentences

Fig. 11: How a paragraph should be written

Cohesion is essential

The orderly progression of chapters, sections and subsections
following a well-conceived outline will show logical
development of the content. Cohesion can be achieved by the
use of:

- *parallel construction* for ideas or equal importance, similar
  functions or similar constituents;

- *transition words* to introduce sentences, to link ideas within the sentence or show relationships within the paragraph;
- *subordination* showing the relative importance of ideas or parts of ideas.

Practices which can destroy cohesion include:

- generalities and vague references using indefinite pronouns – for example: 'many', 'some', 'a lot', 'they';
- repetitive sentence construction – for example always using one type of sentence, or joining ideas with 'and';
- red herrings – for example misplaced, irrelevant or unnecessary ideas.

Clarity helps understanding

Precise, well-balanced sentences should use complex sentence construction to show ideas in relation to each other. Concrete terminology conveys clear meaning. Practices which can destroy clarity are:

- a profusion of simple sentences;
- overuse of expressions such as 'etc.';
- oversimplification;
- misuse of jargon (technical language).

Conciseness sharpens the point

Closely related to clarity is conciseness because clarity is aided by an economy of carefully chosen words – the essence of conciseness. Use a thesaurus in conjunction with a dictionary to choose the most appropriate words. Enemies of conciseness are:

- slang and colloquial expressions – any words which essentially form spoken language;
- superfluous expressions which provide padding to the text – for example: 'Let us now turn to ...', 'It is significant to note the fact that ...';
- pretentious, flowery language or stilted pompous old-fashioned civil service style;
- pedantic inclusion of minute detail;
- words which are too general – for example: 'good', 'well', 'high', 'big'.

Impersonal style raises the register

Most disciplines encourage students to adopt an impersonal style so that the focus is on the research rather than on the researcher. To achieve an impersonal style, avoid:

- the use of 'I', 'we', 'you';
- exclamation marks;
- underlining words in a conversational way for emphasis;
- using a dash instead of a conjunction ('and', 'but', 'for'), a comma or a semi-colon;
- phrasal verbs – for example: 'went up', 'thought well of';
- contractions – for example: 'it's', 'doesn't', 'won't'.

Consistency provides order

The overriding component is consistency because it sets the limits for all the conventions mentioned above. It is essential to establish a format that extends throughout your work because this is a subliminal way of guiding the reader through the text. Therefore, headings, indentations, footnote or endnote format, bibliographic content and format, inclusion of examples and lists all need to be uniform in their presentation.

Redrafting

When your first draft is finished, put it away for 24 hours; you return to it with fresh eyes to see it more objectively – therefore, you are better able to see what changes you need to make. Don't be afraid to revise, but don't overdo it. Research shows that you can alter your initial intention if you redraft too many times.

Hand your edited, proof-read draft to your supervisor for advice on the content. (Editing and proof-reading are discussed separately below.) You may be advised to reorder or add material, to adjust your style, format and grammar. Begin to redraft only after you have discussed the changes or additions which are needed. Remember that the changes you make may affect other parts of the already written text – you must edit those sections too. Don't be discouraged by criticism because it is in your interests to make your thesis as nearly perfect as you can. Many supervisors do not have time to see a thesis more than once. The onus of responsibility is on you to present an acceptable piece of work.

When you are satisfied with your revised draft, submit it to your supervisor as ready for examination.

Adjusting the nuts and bolts

The final adjustments to your script are the activities which will help to ensure that you are delivering a quality product:

- controlling your verbs;
- citing with care;
- editing with judgement;
- proof-reading with precision.

Controlling your verbs

Verbs cause problems unless you control your use of three aspects:

- Choose either present or past tense as your main tense and strive for consistency. The present tense allows you to state principles, definitions and accepted facts. The past tense should be used when a historical perspective is necessary. More complex tenses can be used where the subject matter demands.
- Make sure that all verbs agree in number and person with their subjects. 'Agreement' means that the subject and verb are both in the same form. If a subject is plural then the verb must be plural. Similarly, if one is singular, the other must be singular. Be aware of problem words and phrases such as 'government', 'each', 'either', 'one of the samples' which are singular; and 'data', 'people', 'all', 'both ... and ...' which are plural.
- Make an appropriate choice of mood. English verbs are either *active* or *passive* – that is, their subjects are either *doing the action* or *receiving it*. The passive puts the emphasis on the person or thing receiving the action rather than on the one performing it. A verb in a passive sentence is always a *verb phrase* that includes a form of the verb 'to be' and the past participle of the main verb. The active is the most commonly used mood, but the *passive* is useful for thesis writing when:

  - the subject is unknown, common knowledge or unnecessary;

- the subject and the object need to be reversed for emphasis;
- an awkward referent needs to be avoided (to be sure what is being referred to);
- the use of 'I', 'we', 'you', 'this', 'there' has to be avoided;
- variety of expression is desirable.

The passive is handy, but *don't overuse it* or the text will be limp.

Citing with care

Each institution (sometimes each department) has its own preferred style of citing references. The established guides are:

- Turabian (1973) and Spink (1982) who have made the Chicago Manual of Style accessible;
- the Harvard style used by The Open University;
- Achtert (1985) – the MLA Stylesheet Manual.

Citation of documents from the Internet is also required – however, you must consult your supervisor as to the preferred style. In the Chicago style citations are marked with sequential numbers in the text and footnoted at the bottom of each page in full on the first occurrence. Subsequent references to the same source can be abbreviated (see Turabian or Spink). A full citation for each source must appear in the bibliography. Citing is meticulous work – the important thing to remember is to choose a style and follow it consistently.

Editing with judgement

Editing precedes proof-reading. When editing, you must read each sentence critically to judge that it says what you want it to say. Words and phrases must be in the correct order to convey the precise meaning intended, avoiding ambiguity. You must see that the sentences are complete ideas which move the argument or revelation of the situation forward without contradictions. Paragraphs must be in a logical order. Tables, charts and graphs must appear near the text to which they refer. Irrelevant statements, poor choice of words and unnecessary examples need to be removed. Missing evidence needs to be added. Parallel constructions should occur where necessary. Punctuation should be appropriate to help convey accurate meaning. Check that the sequence of headings is correct, reflects what is in the text and that it makes sense. The conclusion must be a true representative of what has been said.

Editing is a thinking activity in which you are judging objectively what is written.

Proof-reading with precision

The final activity is proof-reading which involves *mechanically reading words* and not ideas, looking for all the typographical errors, misspellings, forgotten and misplaced punctuation and/or correct use of capital letters, noun and verb plurals, formatting, spacing, numbering, widows and orphans. Don't forget that computer spellcheckers allow some howlers.

You are not reading for sense, meaning or ideas when you are proof-reading – you are reading to catch mechanical errors. It is wise to proof-read for formatting errors in a reading separate from that in which you are looking for syntax and grammar errors.

Case studies

Adrian misses the point

Adrian was well motivated, made good progress in the initial stages and was finished well before the deadline. He was very satisfied with his product, feeling as proud as a peacock. As soon as his supervisor started reading the draft, he realised that he would have to approach Adrian in a forthright manner. The long complex sentences with obscure synonyms dredged out of a thesaurus without reference to a dictionary lumbered on. Evidence of plagiarism stood out in the abrupt changes in style.

When Adrian called to see his supervisor to collect his accolades, the mentor drew his attention to the shortcomings and necessary changes. Adrian, affronted by the suggestion of changes, became very defensive – after all, it was *his* research. The supervisor had anticipated the likelihood of an altercation because Adrian had sought minimal guidance from the outset. In the end, a lengthy extension was necessary to allow Adrian time to rewrite.

Janet finds a way

Janet sat surrounded by open books, photocopied journal articles, post-it notes with reminders of other possible references, heaps of dog-eared A4 sheets of notes and downloaded documents from the web. Meticulous planning had been done. Janet had spent days producing sheaves of outlines trying to ensure that all previous work on the topic was included.

Propelled by the urge to get on with the job and not waste time, Janet began to write. She soon realised that she had too much text. She began to cross sections out, editing ruthlessly. Before long, she realised that the changes had blurred the accuracy of the sense initially intended. She was very discouraged by the enormity of the task. A friend suggested that she go back to her notes to colour-code the points following her outlined plan. Janet found that this procedure rescued her from wallowing in detail and helped her to focus on essentials. Her next draft was much improved.

Sian breaks out

Sian is a classic procrastinator. She is so busy with outside activities and in the business of living, that she never gets to the library until an hour before closing time. Becoming aware that time was passing, Sian took hold of herself to try to curtail her delaying tactics. Changing her lifestyle, she amassed a body of respectable notes and a meticulous bibliography. She sat down for a brainstorming session and was able to mind map the main focus.

The discipline she was imposing on herself made her tense but she could see results. She decided to write directly into the word processor from her mind maps. The freedom to add, move or delete text aided her creativity. At the end of each writing session she took a hard copy to proof-read. When she finished a chapter she edited it in the light of the whole. Sian's progress was steady, her supervisor was satisfied, she finished on time and gained a distinction for her thesis.

Discussion points

1. How important is it to begin to write early in the Master's degree programme?
2. What can be gained from reading books and articles about your topic? How much can be said for the view that you have done the research, and you know all there is to know about the subject firsthand.
3. Does everyone attack writing in the same way? Is there one right way?

Questions and answers

Q. I finished my literature review four months ago. My supervisor keeps referring me to newly published journal articles. What should I do?

You need to discuss the most appropriate cut-off point for the inclusion of newly published material with your supervisor. If the articles significantly alter your conclusions then you should certainly include them. However, be sure that you redraft every point that is affected by the new findings in order to maintain consistency. It is important to keep up-to-date, but you may need to weigh up the amount of time required to make all the changes necessary against the wisdom of omitting them.

Q. How important is it for me to write good grammatical English?

In order to express the subtleties of your ideas and your findings, you need to be able to show those relationships through the construction of your sentences as well as by the careful choice of vocabulary. Conversational English does not carry the weight of meaning you need to express. From your reading, you will gain a feeling for the register you need to adopt. You might like to keep a grammar book handy for reference – but you don't need to spend your time reading it from cover to cover.

Q. What are the sections of a thesis?

As might be expected, a scientific thesis and an arts thesis differ in format. The sections which you should expect to have are shown in Figure 12. There are some

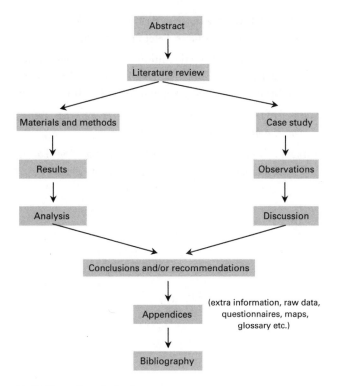

Fig. 12: The sections of a thesis

'official' pages required at the beginning, including a declaration and statements. You will have a title page, maybe a dedication, acknowledgements and a table of contents along with lists of tables and figures.

Bibliography

Achtert, W.S. (1985) *The MLA Style Manual*. MLA.

British Standards Institution (1990) *Recommendations for Citing and Referencing Published Material*, British Standards Institution (2nd editon).

Buzan, T. (1988) *Make the Most of your Mind*. Pan Books.

Eastwood, J. (1994) *Oxford Guide to English Grammar*. Oxford University Press.

Hall, C. (1994) *Getting Down to Writing – A Student's Guide to Overcoming Writer's Block*. Peter Francis Publishers.

Inspiration – professional edition for higher education. Iansyst Training Products, The White House, 72 Fen Road, Cambridge, CB4 1UN. Freephone 0500 141 515.

Spink, J. (1982) *A Manual for Writers of Research Papers, Theses and Dissertations*. Heinemann.

Turabian, K.L. (1973) *A Manual for Writers of Term Papers, Theses and Dissertations*. Chicago University Press.

6

Legal and Moral Issues

Allison Coleman and John Williams

One-minute overview

The aim of this chapter is to enable a student doing research and writing a thesis to use the works of others without breach of copyright or confidentiality laws, and to protect his or her own work against improper use by others.

Students will want to photocopy materials, to quote from the works of others or to use their maps and diagrams in their thesis or any subsequent publications. They may search the Internet and electronic databases and download materials, and they may want to share software. They may carry out questionnaire surveys or interview people. Each of these activities raises copyright and/or confidentiality problems.

In this chapter you will find information and advice on how to deal with these issues under the following headings:
- sources of copyright law;
- the rights that copyright confers;
- the issue of confidentiality;
- case studies;
- discussion points;
- questions and answers.

Sources of copyright law

Before starting – a warning! The law of copyright is complex – it is riddled with exceptions and changes with both the date and the type of work. This chapter is too short to do anything other than highlight issues, so if you think you have a copyright problem you should consult an expert. There is a further reading list at the end of this chapter listing specialist works on copyright which may be of value to you.

The most recent Act of Parliament is the *Copyright, Designs and Patents Act* 1988 (the '1988 Act'), which governs works created after 1 August 1989. However, previous copyright acts are still important and may apply to works created before that date. Also, the 1988 Act applies only to the UK. The laws of other countries may well be different.

The rights that copyright confers

Copyright confers two main sets of rights – *economic* and *moral*. Economic rights enable a copyright owner to earn money. They are the exclusive rights to carry out the following activities:

- copying the work;
- renting or lending the work;
- issuing copies to the public (distributing it);
- performing, playing or showing the work in public;
- broadcasting it or including it in a cable programme;
- making an adaptation of it (e.g. translating it) or to doing any of the above with an adaptation.

Because the rights are exclusive to the owner of copyright, he or she is the only person entitled to do any of the actions listed above. Others need the consent of the copyright owner and consent can be conditional on the payment of a fee. The law is fully up to date and covers doing any of the above by traditional methods or electronically. However, there are a number of very important exceptions to the 1988 Act, known as *permitted acts*. The act most frequently relied on by academic researchers and students is fair dealing for the purposes of research or private study. This legitimises photocopying or downloading of a certain proportion of certain types of copyright works. By way of contrast, when you are writing your thesis or publishing an article you will rely mainly on another exception – that relating to criticism and review. Infringements of copyright and permitted acts are considered further below.

The author of a work also has moral rights:

- the right to be identified as the author or director of a work;
- the right to object to derogatory treatment;
- the right to object to false attribution of a work;
- the right to privacy of certain films and photographs.

Moral rights have become particularly useful to authors whose works are published electronically and are then reproduced in whole or in part without being correctly attributed; or are copied from a database or the Internet and then published in an altered form.

One important limitation on copyright is that it protects only the way in which material is set out – that is its expression. It does not protect the underlying idea. So long as a work is not actually copied, either wholly or substantially, lifting the underlying idea and expressing it in a different way amounts only to *plagiarism*. Plagiarism is a transgression of academic good practice and in committing it a person may breach disciplinary rules, but it does not necessarily involve breach of copyright. Plagiarism can be avoided by adequate footnoting or citation and should not be ignored – each university has a statement on plagiarism and you should find out what yours has to say on the matter.

What do copyright laws protect?

Copyright law protects nine main categories of items, known as 'works'. These are:

- original literary, dramatic, musical or artistic works;
- sound recordings, films, broadcasts or cable programmes;
- the typographical arrangement of published editions.

Many of these categories are further subdivided. 'Literary works', for instance, covers not only books and articles but also 'a table or compilation and … a computer program'. 'Artistic works' covers photographs, diagrams and maps, among other things. Databases are also protected by copyright.

Who owns copyright?

The first owner of copyright in a work is its author – the person who first creates it – but there are also special rules for joint authorship and for works created by employees in the course of their employment. Copyright may be transferred to another person by written assignment, and it also passes by will or intestacy on death. Many publishers require authors to transfer copyright to them in their articles or books under the publishing contract – hence, publishers are commonly the owners of copyright of books and articles. Copyright licences are also common, particularly with software. Here the owner retains copyright but the licensee is given a right to use the software subject to the terms of the licence. This right to use software does not normally authorise giving it to others or allowing them to use it – they should purchase their own.

How long does copyright last?

Under the 1988 Act copyright in literary, dramatic, musical and artistic works lasted for the life of the author plus 50 years. Since 1 January 1996, the copyright term for most of these works has been extended by the *Duration of Copyright Regulations* 1995 (the '1995 Regulations') to life plus seventy years. This means that many works, which had dropped out of copyright, are now once again protected by what is known as 'revived copyright'. The 1995 Regulations are exceptionally complicated and are generally beyond the scope of this chapter. A useful account can be found in Flint et al. (2000).

Infringement of copyright

There are two types of infringement, or breach, of copyright – *primary* and *secondary*. As stated above, the owner of copyright has the exclusive right to copy the work, to rent or to lend it, to issue copies to the public, to perform or show the work in public, to broadcast or include it in a cable programme and to make an adaptation of it. If anyone else does any of these acts without permission, it amounts to primary infringement of copyright. This type of infringement involves breach only of the civil rights of the copyright owner, and it can be committed innocently – there is no need for the infringer to know that the work is protected by copyright, or that their act constitutes infringement. Unlike secondary infringement, primary infringement is not a criminal offence.

The whole work need not be copied, performed etc. for it to amount to a breach of copyright. It is sufficient if a substantial part is used without consent. Copying a section of a work can therefore breach copyright. The test as to whether a part of a work is substantial or not is not just related to the quantity of what is taken, but also takes into account its quality – is it an important part, a key component or a clearly recognisable part? If it is qualitatively important then it doesn't matter that the segment taken is quite small in size in relation to the work as a whole. To some extent the courts work on the principle that if it is worth taking it must be important and so is worth protecting by copyright. This means that the copier has to be very careful. The normal remedies for infringement of the civil rights of a copyright owner are an injunction taken to prevent further breach of the law, or damages for a breach which has already occurred. It should, however, be noted that certain acts will not amount to infringement of copyright. These exceptions are discussed below under the heading of 'permitted acts'. Read this section before you panic about photocopying or downloading!

Secondary infringement of copyright breaches the civil rights of the copyright owner, and is also a criminal offence. Basically it involves *dealing* in copyright works. However, in order to be liable the infringer must have a 'guilty mind' – they must know or have reason to believe that there is a breach of copyright.

Permitted acts

Researchers rely heavily on one particular exception to copyright protection. This is 'fair dealing for the purposes of research or private study' and it enables students and researchers to copy – by photocopying or downloading for example – a proportion of a literary, dramatic, musical or artistic work (but note not other works such as sound recordings) without infringing copyright in it, or, in the case of a published edition, without infringing copyright in the typographical arrangement, which belongs to the publisher.

The governing principle in this particular provision is that the copying must be fair. In America it is known as the 'fair use' provision, a description which is arguably better than our notion of fair dealing. If the copying is of a large proportion of a work or a whole work – for example a whole book – which is in print and available in the bookshops then the use will invariably be unfair and the copying will breach copyright.

Assessing fairness can obviously be quite difficult. Publishers have reached agreements, called licensing agreements, with universities and others which set out what is fair use in their view. Persons who copy within these guidelines will not be sued for infringement of copyright. The terms of these licensing agreements are found in summary form alongside most photocopying machines. Read them and abide by them.

In their writings authors make frequent reference to the works of others. If the ideas of another are used, but not the expression of the other, there can be no breach of copyright for, as stated above, copyright protects the form in which a work is set out and not the underlying ideas. The other author should be cited to avoid allegations of plagiarism, rather than breach of copyright laws.

If an author wishes to quote from the work of another – or to use maps, drawings or tables of another – copyright may be infringed unless the action is permitted under another heading, namely fair dealing for the purposes of criticism or review. The criticism or review may be of the work itself or of a performance of it, and in both cases it must be accompanied by a sufficient acknowledgement. Again the governing principle is that the use (or dealing) must be fair. Basically, it is dangerous to quote large chunks of the work of others – nether does it impress examiners. 'Sufficient acknowledgement' means that the source must be cited in full. Following standard practice for full bibliographic citation should avoid problems. Help is provided on this in Chapter 5 and your supervisor should also be able to advise you.

Various other actions are permitted by the 1988 Act, but they relate mainly to copying by libraries and for the purposes of educational instruction – they are not covered here. They will apply to you only if you also teach in addition to carrying out research.

The issue of confidentiality

Confidentiality is something that we often take for granted. When you go to the doctor you do not expect the content of your 'confidential' consultation to be made public knowledge. You are entitled to rely on your doctor's duty of confidentiality. Of course you can tell others the details of your discussions because the confidentiality belongs to you – but the doctor is prevented from doing so. Much of the law of confidentiality has been developed in relation to the doctor-patient relationship. However, the law extends much further and may embrace some of the research activity undertaken by students.

There are aspects of research that involve the researcher obtaining from another person information that may be of a confidential nature. The most obvious example of this is when you compile a questionnaire and ask members of the public to complete it. Some responses may simply involve interviewees ticking a series of boxes. Others may require free-text answers and the researcher may be centrally involved in obtaining the information and recording the views expressed. Usually interviewee names are not included in the processed data. However, the researcher may often know who an interviewee is and may be privy to sensitive information about their lifestyle, commercially sensitive matters or financial matters. The question arises whether in law such information is subject to a duty of confidence.

The law of confidentiality

The House of Lords in the case of the *Attorney General* v *Guardian Newspapers Ltd* (otherwise known as the 'Spycatcher' case) discussed the law of confidentiality. Lord Goff said that a duty of confidentiality arises in the following circumstances:

- the information concerned is confidential;
- it comes to the knowledge of a person (the confidant) in

circumstances where he or she had notice, or is held to have agreed, that the information is confidential, with the effect that it would be just that he or she would be precluded from disclosing the information;

- it is in the public interest that the confidentiality should be protected.

Clearly information is not confidential when it is already in the public domain. The information may be a matter of public record – for example, the performance of a publicly quoted company – or the individual may have previously made it public.

The duty arises in a number of different relationships. Perhaps the most common application of the duty of confidentiality is in the doctor–patient relationship. However, it may also arise out of a contract. This may be of particular interest to research students who are funded by a commercial, public or voluntary undertaking. The agreement may well contain a duty to keep certain types of information confidential. Such a contractual term has important implications for a research student who intends that his or her work will be disseminated as widely as possible. If faced with such a clause it is essential to be clear about how extensive any restrictions on publication may be. Do not be afraid to raise this with the body concerned before you actually start your research. Where an issue of confidentiality does arise, most universities have a system whereby a bar on access to a thesis can be granted for reasons of confidentiality – it might be worth finding out about this as it could mean the difference between proceeding with research or not.

Particular issues need to be addressed when interviewing people. In fairness to those who agree to give up their time to fill in your questionnaire or to be interviewed by you, it is important that there is agreement on the issue of confidentiality. Is the interview confidential? Does the person agree to their remarks being attributed to them in your thesis? Can you use the information they provided or did they intend it to be used only as background information? Are there times during the interview when they wish to go 'off the record'?

Do they demand the right to 'check the accuracy' of your use of the information provided?

The important principle here is that issues surrounding confidentiality must be resolved *prior* to the interview taking place. Unless both parties agree at the outset whether or not the interview is confidential, and if so to what extent, then problems may arise.

Can legal confidences ever be broken?

As can be seen from the 'Spycatcher' case, the public interest must support the confidentiality. This suggests that there may be situations where public interest demands that a confidence is broken. Confidentiality is not an absolute principle and the law recognises this. In the case of W v *Egdell* in Kennedy and Grubb (2000) the court allowed a doctor to break a doctor-patient confidence. The question was whether a confidential report on the mental health of the patient could be disclosed to the Home Office on the grounds of public safety. The court said that it had to balance on the one hand the public interest in maintaining the confidential nature of the doctor–patient relationship, and on the other the public interest in public safety. After considering these competing interests the court came down in favour of disclosure – the public safety argument outweighed the doctor–patient argument. However, this is not always the case. In another case (the names aren't given here to protect the confidentiality of those involved in the case!) it was decided that the public interest in doctor–patient confidentiality outweighed the public interest in knowing that two doctors diagnosed as HIV positive were continuing to practice.

Where a confidence can be broken under the principle outlined in *Egdell* it is important that any disclosure is restricted to those who, in pursuit of the public interest, need to know.

Social science researchers may encounter such dilemmas when undertaking interviews. It is possible that a rapport will be built up between the interviewer and the interviewee and the former may become a confidant for the latter. This can create difficult ethical and legal problems, especially if evidence of child abuse or the abuse of a vulnerable adult is disclosed. In deciding whether a disclosure should be made it is essential to consider the public interest dimension. Such decisions should be discussed with your supervisor or some other person – being careful not to identify the confidant during these preliminary discussions. Researchers may also become aware of other forms of criminal activity during their research.

Police access to confidential information

The *Police and Criminal Evidence Act* 1984 allows the police to have access to certain categories of confidential information, subject to satisfying the safeguards contained in the act. These provisions are used in only a few cases. Nevertheless it is important not to forget that access may be possible.

Ethical considerations

Although information in your possession may not have been obtained in accordance with the statement of Lord Goff in 'Spycatcher', some thought should be given to the ethics of disclosure. The fact that there is no legal duty of confidentiality does not always make it 'right' to disclose. Researchers should be sensitive to issues such as the privacy of the individual and also to the consequences of disclosure to the individual and his or her family. Ethical considerations are just as important as legal ones.

Case studies

Tim gets it all wrong

Tim is working hard on his thesis. He has read widely, photocopied everything he can lay his hands on and downloaded all the materials the Internet and on-line databases can provide. He and his friends are overawed by the huge quantity of materials he has built up.

When Tim starts to write, he finds that he really cannot improve on what other authors have already written, so he decides to cut and paste from their works and to string it all together in narrative form. Working right up until the deadline he doesn't have time to add footnotes to any of the sources he has used. He hands his first chapter to his supervisor. He is horrified to find that after all his hard work his supervisor accuses him of lacking originality, of plagiarism and infringement of copyright.

Bethany bites the dust

Bethany heard of Tim's problems but thinks she can pull the wool over her supervisor's eyes by finding an obscure out-of-print book that is not in the library of her home university. The book is so good she feels that she cannot improve on its mode of expression or analysis. Bethany copies out most of the, rather small, book and submits it as her thesis. Just to be on the safe side – so she thinks – she includes the book in her bibliography.

Unknown to her, her supervisor is a personal friend of the author and has read the book and so recognises it instantly. Bethany finds herself being interviewed by the same unfair practice panel as Tim and she too faces allegations of infringement of copyright.

Good old Tom!

Tom decides to read widely before spending money on photocopying and printing. He adds to his bibliography each item he reads and notes its importance for his research. By the time he starts to write, his files are very much thinner than Tim's but he knows his subject thoroughly and has developed his own ideas. He draws on the work of others but explains their views in his own words, using quotations sparingly and footnoting a reference to each book, article etc. that he has used when developing a point. Tom's supervisor, who is a little jaded after reading the work by Tim and Bethany, is delighted and tells Tom that he has a bright future as a researcher.

Sian's dilemma – to tell or not to tell?

Sian is working on her PhD on the incidence of poverty in remote rural areas. Part of her research involves visiting people in their own homes and asking them a series of questions relating to their income, housing conditions and health. The nature of the questions, and Sian's ability to put people at their ease, means that many people divulge very personal information. Sian tells all the interviewees that the interview is confidential and that that they will not be identifiable in the final report. One such interview takes place with Catrin, a thirty-year-old mother of two young children. She lives with her partner, Aled, who is the father of one of the children. When discussing health, Catrin discloses that Aled is violent towards her on occasions. The last time this occurred, Catrin had to go to the accident and emergency unit of the local hospital for treatment. She told the hospital that she had fallen down the stairs. Although the medical staff did not believe her, they felt there was nothing they could do. Sian is horrified by this information and fears for Catrin's safety, and for that of the children. However, she is also aware that she has given an undertaking of confidentiality and that to disclose this information to the police would be a breach of that duty. What should she do? Is there anything that Sian could do before the interviews to avoid this kind of ethical dilemma?

Discussion points

1. How can copyright be reconciled with freedom of information?
2. Does copyright give too much protection to the owners of rights at the expense of users of information?
3. To what extent does copyright apply in the digital environment?
4. Is the duty of confidentiality ever absolute?
5. How should you balance the competing public interests in the duty of confidentiality and the need to break the duty in certain circumstances?
6. Would you ever feel able to keep a confidence when you know that a third party may be injured unless you disclose the information?
7. What kind of information should be capable of being protected by the duty of confidentiality?

Questions and answers

Q. *Does copyright apply to everything I use and write?*

The safest answer to this question is yes, unless you are using very old material. Most students other than those researching historical matters can therefore assume that all of the laws discussed in this chapter apply.

Q. *Where can I get advice on copyright?*

Many universities and institutes of higher education have copyright officers. Contact your registry for the name of this person. Other sources of advice are industrial liaison offices or open/distance learning units.

Q. *Can I afford to take risks?*

No!

Q. *How should I go about trying to resolve the difficult dilemma of whether or not to break a confidence?*

It is crucial that you identify the reasons for your ultimate decision clearly (whether it be to disclose or to reveal the information). Making a record of your reasoning is sensible. It often helps to discuss the ethical dilemma with somebody else who you can trust (such as your supervisor) but remember not to disclose, directly or indirectly, the identity of the beneficiary of the confidentiality. Ultimately it is your decision so be convinced in your own mind that you can defend what you decide to do.

Q. *Can an aggrieved person bring a legal action against me for breach of confidence?*

Yes.

Q. *If I decide to break a confidence and can justify it as being in the public interest, does this mean that the information is now in the public domain and I can use it freely?*

No. If you decide to disclose in the public interest, you must only disclose it to those people who need to know the information – for example the police or the social services.

Bibliography

Flint, M.F., Fitzpatrick, N. and Thorne, C. (2000) *A User's Guide to Copyright*, 4th edition. Butterworths.

Kennedy, I. and Grubb, A. (2000) *Medical Law*. 3rd edition. Butterworths. Chapter 8.

Additional helpful material

Darley, B., Griew, A., McLoughlin, K. and Williams, J. (1994) *How to keep a Clinical Confidence*. HMSO.

Farrington, D. (1998) *The Law of Higher Education*, 2nd edition. Butterworths. pp. 512–13.

Garnet, K., Rayner James, J. and Davies, G. (1999) *Copinger and Skone James on Copyright*, 14th edition. Sweet and Maxwell.

Laddie, H., Prescott, I. and Vittoria, M. (2000) *The Modern Law of Copyright*, 3rd edition. Butterworths.

Padfield, T. (2001) *Copyright for Archivists and Users of Archives*. Public Record Office.

7 Understanding Submission and Examination Processes

Gina Preston

One-minute overview

This chapter will explain what is usually involved in submitting a thesis. Actual practice varies widely from one institution to another and the aim is to point out questions you need to address and when you might need to address them. It is vital that you find out what the exact situation is for you at your university.

The chapter covers the following issues:

■ submitting your thesis – when should it be submitted, in what format and to whom?

■ assessing the thesis – who assesses it?

■ post-assessment issues – what happens if you fail?

■ case studies;

■ discussion points;

■ questions and answers.

Submitting your thesis

Thoughts of submitting your thesis, or even of your writing up are not likely to be at the forefront of your mind until you approach the end of your research. However, it is important that you do spend some time fairly early on sorting out what you have to do and when you need to do it. This will help you to establish a schedule that you can stick to and ensure that you are not rushing around at the last moment tying up loose administrative ends – when you may desperately need those extra few days to finalise the thesis itself.

Many institutions have very clear rules and a thesis submitted at the wrong time or in the wrong format will simply not be considered no matter how wonderful a piece of research it is.

Figure 13 shows a flow chart illustrating the questions you need to find answers to before you start writing your thesis.

These questions will be considered in turn now.

Finding the submission procedures

If you are at a university which puts the needs of its students as a priority, and has a commitment to the provision of

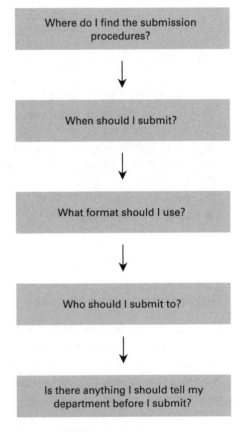

Fig. 13: Questions you should find the answers to

quality information, then you should have been provided with a booklet at the beginning of your course explaining the submission procedure. Such booklets are becoming more widely available. Alternatively, your institution may hold induction sessions to explain what you should do. If your institution provides neither of these, ask why not.

If there is no booklet or induction session, you will have to find out the answers to these questions yourself. Try your supervisor to start with. Find out who the key people are in your university administration, get hold of a copy of the university regulations – these may not be easy to read but the information will be there.

Whether you are given a booklet or not, it will be helpful for you to look at what others have done. Go to the library and take a look at theses that have been written recently in your subject area – look at the format and style. However, be wary of following this approach without checking that regulations have not changed.

When can I submit?

All institutions have time limits for submission of theses. In general, most full-time Master's courses are of between 12 and 24 months duration, the first 9 or 12 months of which will be the taught element, with a further 3–15 months for writing the thesis.

You should have been informed of the exact timetable for your particular course either when you were offered a place or during the first few sessions. If, for whatever reason, this is not the case then you should find out now. If you miss the deadline for submission, the excuse that someone told you the wrong information is not likely to be taken seriously. It is your job to ensure that you know what is required.

In what format should my thesis be submitted?

Universities vary significantly in their strictness concerning the presentation of theses, even in such fundamental issues as word length. In some instances, different departments within an institution have requirements that differ to some extent. Three key questions will be examined here.

How long can/should the thesis be?

Word limits vary widely both between institutions and within institutions themselves. If your thesis is in an arts or humanities subject, you can usually expect the word length to be longer than in science subjects – the latter commonly involve a significant practical project and require fewer actual words.

Expect to find a limit of between 10,000 and 20,000 words – although in some cases it could be as few as 4,000 or as many as 50,000. Bear in mind that *maximum* word lengths are usually what are given and your supervisor should be able to advise you as to what would be appropriate for your particular project.

How should the thesis look?

Many universities have clearly laid out regulations telling you about some or all of the following:

- type of paper
- typeface
- font size
- margins
- line spacing
- how to caption figures and tables.

In all cases it will be expected that your thesis is typewritten or word processed. If you are having your thesis typed or if you are doing it yourself ensure that you follow these regulations from the beginning. It is much harder to go back and reformat it at the end.

How should the thesis be presented?

Generally it will be expected that your thesis is presented in soft binding. At some institutions you will be expected to arrange this yourself, at others it may be done for you. In addition, you will have to ensure that you follow the institution house style with regard to:

- title page
- contents
- references
- footnotes
- page numbering

- division into chapters
- glossaries
- summaries and abstracts
- number of copies to submit.

To whom should I submit my thesis?

In many cases the thesis can be submitted in the first instance to your supervisor, the course director or the course administrator. Do check, particularly if you intend to post your thesis to a named person, that this is the right person and that they will be able to pick up the package after delivery.

You will also need to know what administrative forms need to be submitted with your thesis. Usually you will need to present a summary of approximately 300 words and complete a presentation form in which you sign a declaration, supported by your supervisor, that states to what degree the research is your own work and that the same work has not been submitted for any other degree. Your university is also likely to require proof that you have paid all your fees and you may need to obtain a statement from the finance office to that effect.

It is vital that you complete all the required forms and submit them at the right time to avoid any delays in the examination of your thesis. Institutions may require the forms to be presented some time before the thesis is submitted in order to enable them to find an appropriate external examiner.

Informing your departments of problems

If you feel there are any matters which have adversely affected the preparation of your thesis, it is vital that these are drawn to the attention of your supervisor or head of department at the earliest opportunity. You will need to provide any medical notes relating such circumstances when you submit your thesis. If you have had problems with your supervision, this must have been drawn to the attention of your head of department before submission if it is to be considered as a mitigating factor.

In many institutions, candidates are allowed to suspend their studies if exceptional circumstances arise – such as ill health or severe financial hardship. In these cases the submission date would be put back by the length of the suspension, usually up to a maximum of a year. In most other cases you will be expected to submit on time and your thesis will not be considered if you do not meet the deadline.

Assessing the thesis

Now you have finally handed your thesis in you can sit back and relax for a bit. There is nothing you can actively do at this stage, but you will probably find it helpful to have some idea of what is happening to your work, and when you can expect to hear whether you have been successful or not. If you expect to have an oral examination (viva), you can go over your thesis looking for alterations you might like to make – this will be helpful preparation.

The examination procedures

Each university will have a clearly laid down examination procedure for each course that it runs – this should be set out in your course handbook. The procedure at your university will involve:

- internal examination only;
- external examination only;
- both internal and external examination.

A viva may be involved in any of these three procedures.

Internal examination only

The role of the internal examiner is to decide if your work and knowledge meet the standard normally expected of a student in your department who was submitting for the same degree, and if it meets the university's criteria for the award of the degree. This can be done in a number of ways:

- your supervisor alone may determine your mark;
- another member of your department or institution who has not been involved in your supervision may mark your work;
- your supervisor and another member of your department or institution may read your thesis and agree a mark;

However the mark is decided, it may be subject to approval by an examination board.

External examination only

An appropriate person, with experience in the field, from outside the institution will have been selected as your external examiner (your supervisor may well act as external examiner for a course in another institution). External examiners are usually paid a small sum for this service and are given a clear deadline for return of the thesis, and usually a copy of the university regulations so they know whether or not your thesis is sound from a subject point of view and also that it meets the word limits and formatting criteria.

The external examiner will normally have only your thesis on which to base the mark, will not have discussed it with your supervisor and will judge it on its merits. The role of the examiner is to determine if your thesis achieves the appropriate academic standards, and that you have achieved a standard comparable to that of a student being examined for the same degree in the same academic discipline in another university.

Internal and external examination

Two examiners will assess your work, one from inside your institution and one from outside. They will look at your thesis independently and reach a joint result. If, as rarely happens, agreement is not reached then it is usual for a second external examiner to be elected to consider your research. The examiners usually have equal status in examining you and your work – however, on a difficult academic issue more weight may be placed on the advice of the external examiner, who can offer a more independent view of your case.

Post-assessment issues

When you receive your results, hopefully you will be in a position to celebrate. You might want to consider publishing your work or going on to do further research such as a doctorate. However, many candidates don't find themselves in this position immediately. You may receive one of the following results, although you should bear in mind that in different institutions the process can be more straightforward or more complex.

You have passed

It is usual at Master's level to obtain a straight pass. However, universities are increasingly introducing some grading scheme or other – such as distinction, merit or pass. You would normally have to achieve exceptionally high marks, often in both the taught examinations and the thesis, to obtain a distinction (usually over 70%).

Minor amendments required

This is still a very encouraging result. You will be given clear instructions as to what amendments need to be made and a short deadline in which to carry them out. These are usually typographical in nature.

Oral interview (viva)

The majority of institutions do not require Master's students to attend a viva. However, practice varies and some conduct a viva for borderline candidates, or even a majority of candidates. You will not know why you have been asked to attend a viva, but it is important to understand that if you are a borderline candidate, your percentage mark can only stay the same or improve as a result of the viva. You should be positive and be ready to explain where you think you could have done a better job in retrospect.

Resubmission

In this case the examiners consider that your thesis demonstrates original work and could be amended to be worthy of a Master's degree. Usually they will identify some fundamental flaws in the research and you will be required to address these and resubmit within a given longer time period, usually between 6 and 12 months. A resubmission fee will probably be required – usually £50–£100. If you prefer you can decide not to resubmit and settle for a diploma instead.

Failure

The examiners have determined that your thesis does not meet the academic standards for the Master's course and that they cannot award the degree. In most cases, provided your taught course examination results were satisfactory, you would still be eligible for a diploma. You have the right of appeal against such a decision.

Appealing against your examination result

If you feel that your examination was not fair or that extenuating circumstances have not been considered, you can appeal against the result. Unless your appeal is related to the quality of your supervision, your supervisor is probably the best person to help and advise you at this time and to ensure that your appeal is realistic. Most universities have well-established appeals procedures which will either be in your departmental handbook or available from your departmental office or university central administration.

Determining your right to appeal

Usually an appeal will only be considered in the following circumstances:

- You can show that the examination procedure was not carried out appropriately and that this is likely to have affected the examiners' judgement – for example, your thesis was sent to an inappropriate external examiner or was delayed in some way.
- There were exceptional circumstances – such as ill health, bereavement or poor supervision – which affected your thesis and of which the examiners were not aware. You should have informed your examination convener of this when you submitted. If you did and the information was not considered, or if you can show good reasons why the information was not provided, you would have grounds for appeal.
- One or more of the examiners did not carry out an adequate assessment, or was biased or prejudiced for some reason. This is very hard to prove.

Appeals should not be entered into lightly as they will take a lot of time and energy on your part and that of your supervisor. Ensure that you are being realistic about whether your failure really was unreasonable.

In many cases you will have to act quickly and make an appeal within a short time – occasionally as little as a week, although most places allow at least a month. Appeals are considered at a very senior level, often by a vice-chancellor, before being referred to a committee for consideration. This can take some time and you may be called on to provide further evidence to support your appeal. You will probably have the opportunity to attend an appeal hearing.

The results of an appeal

The outcome of your appeal will be sent to you formally in writing. The possible outcomes are:

- rejection of the appeal – a decision you would have to accept;
- permission to revise the thesis and resubmit it for examination – usually where you received incorrect administrative advice on presentation or where a complaint about poor supervision was upheld.
- resubmission of the thesis for re-examination in its present form, ensuring that the examiners are now aware of any extenuating circumstances of which they were not informed before. In most cases, new examiners would be appointed and they may or may not be aware that they are undertaking a re-examination. It is usual in these cases for both the original and the new examiners' reports to then be considered by the examination board.

Case studies

Russell burns the midnight oil

Russell has progressed erratically during the writing-up period – sometimes producing large volumes of work between meetings with his supervisor, and at other times avoiding the meetings so as not to have to face up to his lack of progress. The submission deadline is marked clearly on his calendar and he has a pile of notes from his supervisor urgently requesting a meeting to look at the final draft. Russell looks at them all woefully as he finalises next season's rugby schedule on his computer.

Eventually, two weeks before the deadline, his supervisor corners him in the coffee shop and drags Russell back to fetch his disks. The supervisor is surprised that the final draft is nearly finished and that the quality of the work is better than might have been expected. However, Russell has thrust the departmental handbook underneath a leg of his desk to stop it wobbling, and has not consulted the regulations on format and presentation. His supervisor helpfully draws Russell's attention to the relevant sections and draws up an action plan to enable him to meet the submission deadline.

Russell spends most of the next fortnight at his computer day and night, finalising his content and reformatting the part he had already completed. The rugby schedule is thrust under the leg of the table in place of the handbook and his mates are amazed when he does not turn up for training.

Russell hands in his thesis the day before the deadline. The examiners agree that the thesis is academically sound and it is referred back to him for minor amendments, although the examiners do comment that the use of a spellchecker would have been beneficial.

David goes his own way

David presents the final draft of his thesis to his supervisor a month before the deadline. He has typed it himself and paid meticulous attention to the university regulations regarding presentation. However, despite the numerous occasions on which his supervisor has tried to redirect his thinking and suggested restructuring and considering new material, David has decided to stick to his original plan.

The supervisor once again makes a number of suggestions but at this late stage, even if David were prepared to consider changes, they would be too extensive to make in time. David goes away and makes a few minor corrections to appease his supervisor, handing in the thesis in well in advance of the deadline.

Both the external and internal examiner are agreed that the thesis does not represent the standard of work required and that there are basic flaws in the research. David is invited to undertake major amendments and resubmit his thesis within a year.

Catherine gets nervous

One month before the deadline for submission, Catherine rather nervously carts her final draft along to her supervisor. She leaves the dissertation with him and goes home and tries very unsuccessfully not to think about whether he is at that minute reading it and what he thinks about it.

At the end of the week, even more nervously, she knocks on his door and is invited in. The supervisor has been through the thesis in detail and makes a few suggestions as to improvements in style and things that could be added or omitted. Catherine is rather embarrassed that the supervisor is so glowing in his praise of the final draft and goes back to do the amendments with renewed vigour.

Catherine's thesis is submitted one week before the deadline and she decides to go and stay with friends for a week or so to recover from the hard work and stress. Soon after she returns, the result comes through to say that she has passed. Her supervisor says that she narrowly missed obtaining a distinction and he strongly urges her to consider further research in the field.

Discussion points

1. Before beginning your writing up, what actions do you think you could take to save you time and help you to comply with your university regulations and submit the thesis in the right format on time?
2. Do you know what happens at your university after you have submitted your thesis? How long do you have to wait for a result? How are you informed?
3. What happens at your university if you do not pass first time? What right of appeal do you have? Do you think the procedure is fair?

Questions and answers

Q. *I have not been given any written information regarding the submission of my thesis. I am about to begin writing up and need to know what is required. My supervisor is very vague about the regulations. Who should I approach?*

Now is definitely the time to get this information. Go to your department or faculty office first and see if they have some documentation. Failing that, maybe your university has a graduate school? If you have no luck with any of these you will have to call on your university administration and get a copy of the university regulations and examine these in detail. If your university does not provide helpful documentation, report this to your student representative. If people do not complain things may never get better.

Q. *I have not been happy with my supervision and this has made work on my dissertation much more difficult than for others on the course. I feel that this may have adversely affected my thesis. What can I do?*

Your university should have an established procedure for dealing with this and it is important that you find out about this straight away. Ask in your departmental office or make an appointment to see your head of department. Steps you might take are listed below:

- speak informally about your concerns to your supervisor;
- make an appointment to see your head of department;
- if the supervisor is the problem a new one could be found at this stage;
- a formal procedure can be instigated which would usually involve you making a written complaint;
- your complaint may be considered by the examiners when your thesis is examined – do not leave making a complaint until you receive the results of your thesis.

Q. *I have been invited to attend a viva examination. Why I have been singled out and what can I expect?*

There is no need to worry about an oral examination. Your supervisor may be able to explain why you have been selected. It could be for one of a number of reasons, such as:

- the examiners are required to viva a sample of candidates from the course and you were chosen at random;
- your result is borderline in some way – it could be close to a distinction, for example;
- the mark you received was equal to the average for your course and, therefore, you make a good marker for the external examiner to refer to when carrying out vivas for borderline cases in your group.

An oral examination is nothing to worry about but naturally you should prepare thoroughly for it. Re-read your thesis and ensure you are up to date on any recent developments in the field. The purpose of the examination will be to test your general knowledge of the field and to question you on matters of detail arising from your thesis. It is an opportunity for you to discuss your work with two specialists in the field – make the most of it!

8 Explaining how to Publish

Alan Bond

One-minute overview

Publishing makes your research more accessible than if it were constrained to two copies of a thesis based at the institution where it was written. At the same time it will give you an advantage over your peers who have also gained a Master's level degree.

This chapter explains how to go about publishing your research and is structured under the following headings:

■ deciding whether you want to publish;
■ deciding where you want to publish;
■ understanding the supervisor's role in publishing;
■ understanding the publishing process;
■ case studies;
■ discussion points;
■ questions and answers.

Deciding whether you want to publish

You're either about to finish or have finished your Master's thesis, so why would you want to think about publishing? It is worth pointing out that if you are keen to get your name into print for whatever reason, the sooner you get things in motion the better. Why? Because research is not novel for long. If you don't publish your discoveries, someone else somewhere in the world will make the same discovery – albeit after you, but they'll get all the credit. A more practical reason is that your research will still be fresh in your mind and you'll find it easier to change the format of your work to suit that required by your chosen publishers, and to respond to the comments of reviewers where appropriate.

Why might you want to publish?

A number of possible, equally valid, reasons why you might wish to publish your research work are:

- you fancy a career as an academic;
- you feel that your research is important and that other people should have easy access to it;
- you feel that publishing is the obvious next step after your Master's degree;
- you want to get your name known;
- you simply want to see if you can;
- it will help your CV as it will demonstrate the value of your research and that you are capable of being proactive and getting more from your Master's experience than the average student.

The actual reason may be a combination of these.

Deciding where you want to publish

Before you can decide where to publish, you need to have worked out the reasons for publishing. The number of published journals has increased over the years and, from the point of view of publishing, this has good and bad points. There is more likely to be a journal publishing in your field of research, which should make it much easier to find a journal in which to place your article. However, it means you will have to look through a lot of journals to make sure you have found the most appropriate one.

What are the possibilities?

There are three types of publication for which you may like to aim.

- *Peer review journal* – this is a journal published periodically which will ask a number of referees (normally at least two) to review articles submitted for publication to check whether the research is suitable material. A peer review journal will normally have a limited distribution to libraries, academics and companies that subscribe.

The length of articles varies, but they are typically about 5,000 words.

- *Journal/magazine with no peer review* – these tend to be published more frequently than peer review journals and usually have a much larger circulation (in the thousands). Articles from such publications do get referenced by other workers. The lengths of articles vary, but are typically around 2,000 words.
- *Book or book chapter* – the advice at this point would be not to run before you can walk! Most book publishers would prefer you to have some experience of publishing journal articles before you take on a book.

What is appropriate?

Table 11 will help to narrow down the sort of journal you should be looking for. It is based on a consideration of the possible reasons for publishing combined with the possible outlets listed above.

A common approach these days is to submit an article for a peer review journal and also a shorter article for a magazine with a wider circulation. This way, the research is reported and checked by your peers, and your name is recognised by a wider audience. It should be stressed at this point that once a magazine/journal has accepted your paper it owns copyright and you cannot submit the same article elsewhere. For this reason, care has to be taken in writing more than one article from the same piece of research.

Understanding the supervisor's role in publishing

Assuming that you have never published before, your supervisor can help you a lot and may be able to:

- give useful advice;
- edit draft copies for you;
- co-write the paper.

Don't be afraid of suggesting the last of these – your supervisor's career depends on publishing papers and, time

Reasons why you might want to publish	What are the possibilities?
You fancy a career as an academic	You should be aiming for a peer review journal because publication in these is necessary for a successful research career within the academic world
You feel that your research is important and that other people should have easy access to it	Research which is published in a peer review journal is taken more seriously by colleagues than non-refereed work – however, publication in a more popular publication reaches a wider audience
You feel that publishing is the obvious next step after your Master's degree	For an academic, this is true – if this is the career you intend to pursue, then go for a peer review journal; if not, then try to think of why it is an obvious step for you and then refer to this table again
You want to get your name known	Any sort of publication will get your name known, but you should think about the reasons why you want to get your name known to narrow it down more – one possibility is to publish in both a peer review journal and in a non-reviewed journal
You simply want to see if you can	It is harder to publish in a peer review journal – how much of a challenge do you want?
It will help your CV as it will demonstrate the value of your research and that you are capable of being proactive and getting more from your Master's experience than the average student	Your CV will be helped by any sort of publication, but to get the most out of your CV you should think about how you are going to use it and where you will send it – then look at the appropriate category in this table

▲
Table. 11
Choosing where
to publish

permitting, they may be very pleased to get involved. If this does happen you should still be the first-named author on the submitted paper because it was your research, and work at this stage by the supervisor is not likely to involve anything like the time you spent on the original research.

On behalf of supervisors, I would also recommend that you acknowledge the time they've put in to helping you in your work. If their input has really helped to shape the research or paper, then they do deserve to be a co-author. If they have simply been able to offer good advice at the right time without becoming heavily involved then an acknowledgement in the paper itself would not go amiss.

Understanding the publishing process

This section takes you through a sequence of steps that you should follow to identify a suitable journal for publishing in and to put the article in the appropriate format. The sequence is summarised in Figure 14.

Make sure that the journal is interested in what you have to offer

Contact the editor by email, fax, letter or phone. The editor is likely to be an academic who works on the journal part-time, along with lecturing and research responsibilities. As such, editors tend to be very approachable, and if they feel that your potential article is unsuited to their journal then they may well have suggestions for more suitable outlets.

Copy the notes for authors

Most journals have a section entitled 'notes for authors' in each issue. Sometimes they aren't found in the journal itself but can be obtained from the editor, publishers, or, more commonly, a journal web page. For example, notes for authors can be found on the web pages of:

- the *Journal of Environmental Planning and Management* – www.tandf.co.uk/journals/carfax/09640568.html

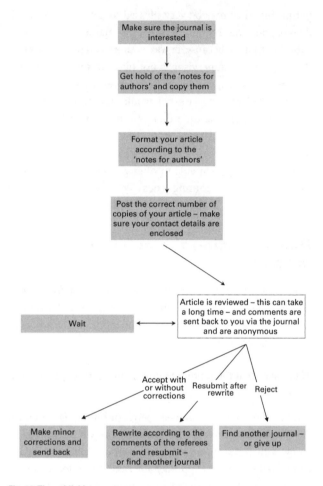

Fig. 14: The publishing process

- the *Journal of Environmental Management* – www.elsevier
  .com/locate/issn/0301-4797

Photocopy the appropriate notes for authors and follow them when preparing your article. The journal may require electronic submission or you may find that a paper copy of the article is required to be double-spaced, single-sided and that several copies are required – sometimes with additional copies of the summary on its own. If separate summaries are required, these will be for the journal to send to potential reviewers asking if they can and are interested in reviewing your article. Now you should understand the reason for having contacted the journal early to see if they were interested in publishing. If you start at this stage, formatting your article accordingly and making all the copies and then find that the subject areas don't match, that's a lot of wasted time and money.

Format your article according to the notes for authors

Don't underestimate the amount of time this may take – a diagram or table you spent days preparing may need redrawing if you are required to change its line spacing! If you continue to write articles in the future, this problem will occur less frequently as you will prepare all your diagrams and tables in a more appropriate format for publishing.

Send your article to the address specified in the notes for authors

Make sure that you have enclosed the correct number of copies of everything you were asked for. This may have included an electronic copy of your work. Don't forget to enclose a covering letter with your contact details.

Wait!

After you have submitted, you can do nothing but wait while the following stages are being worked through:

- the journal checks that your article is within their remit;
- the journal finds referees;
- the referees review your article;
- the journal posts the reviews to you.

What happens in each of these stages is discussed in more detail below.

The journal checks that your article is within their remit

After the journal receives your proposed article they check that the subject matter is appropriate. If something goes wrong at this stage and the editor feels that the article is inappropriate and sends it back, this does not mean that it isn't publishable. It means that the editor feels that the subject of the article does not fit within the remit of the journal. You should approach a different journal.

The journal finds referees

What is more likely to happen is that two of the article – which you will probably have supplied yourself – will be sent to different referees with expertise in the subject area covered by the article. You should realise that there are many journals and only a limited number of experts. To be eligible to review a journal article simply requires that a person has published in the field themselves, hence the journal will be aware of their existence.

The referees review your article

The reviewers each receive your article with some instructions sent by the journal for reviewing it. Typically these will include:

- a proposed deadline for review – commonly about four weeks;
- criteria for evaluation – for example the quality and content of the research, quality brevity and clarity of presentation, along with significance, relevance and timeliness of the topic;
- a list of recommendations for the reviewer to choose from, such as:
  - acceptance
  - acceptance with minor revisions
  - acceptance subject to more significant changes
  - rejection but with re-evaluation after major revisions
  - rejection.

The reviewers complete a short report stating their recommendation detailing how the article fares against the criteria. They send this back to the journal.

The journal posts the reviews to you

The journal will wait until they have all reviews before writing to you with copies of the reports – you will never know who reviewed your article.

It is not uncommon to wait six months – it depends on how quickly the administration of the journal works and on when the referees can find the time to review the article. Most reviewers are busy and often leave the job until the last minute! When you do get your reviewer comments back, you should bear in mind that however good it is there will always be altered items! In fact, if your supervisor has read through any of your work more than once, you may have found that they altered something you had written on the first edit, and then changed it back to how it was on the second edit! This is pointed out because there are likely to be a number of issues highlighted by the reviewers which they feel need changing. You will also probably find that the reviewers don't agree with each other, which makes it very difficult for you to make sensible changes – and it is not uncommon for one reviewer to accept an article and another to reject it. The journal editor will decide to accept or reject the article based on their recommendations.

Make changes

The reviews you receive will explain what work needs to be done in order to edit the article so that it can be published. Make the changes but do not compromise your beliefs in doing this – everyone is entitled to a view and you should only make changes that you agree with. At the same time, don't be too protective of your work – the referees are experienced people and will have suggested changes for good reasons.

Case studies

Russell considers the merits of publication

Russell was happy to have been awarded an MA and began to become a little concerned about his future. He did not have a job lined up and hadn't really felt the need to think about it previously. Now he was faced with unemployment and he began to wonder whether publishing his Master's thesis might give him an edge in the job market. At the same time, he had no desire to go anywhere near his research again. He felt that it had been an enormous weight off his shoulders when he finished writing his thesis and had submitted it – why would he want to start again?

He eventually decided that 'needs must' and went to see his supervisor who encouraged him strongly to try and publish – the supervisor even offered to help edit the paper. They agreed a deadline for the first draft to be given to the supervisor. However, Russell found it hard to motivate himself to produce a draft – there always seemed to be something more interesting to do. After several months, his supervisor called him to tell him that he had just been asked to referee a paper for a journal which superseded the research Russell had carried out – it was too late!

David tries to salvage his job prospects

Having been asked to resubmit his thesis, David was worried about the job offer being held for him by the firm he had worked for during his year in industry. He saw the idea of publishing as a way of proving to his potential employees that his research was indeed of good quality. With this in mind, he went to the library and picked out a very well known and respected international journal and looked through it to find if there were any details on submitting papers. He couldn't find any so he noted the address of the editor.

He then spent some weeks rewriting his thesis in the light of the report he had received from the examiner, who he felt had been pedantic. Having done this, he filed away his rewritten thesis because he wasn't permitted to resubmit until 6 months had gone by, and sent two copies of the same document to the editor of the journal. Judging by what he'd heard about publishing, he expected to hear from the referees at about the same time that he resubmitted his thesis.

He was a little shocked to find his paper sent back to him after two weeks, with a polite letter explaining that the journal did not have time to consider articles submitted in an inappropriate format, and that it was about four times too long anyway.

Catherine grows in confidence

Having successfully obtained her Master's degree, Catherine really started to believe in her own abilities. She was excited about the prospect of publishing her work and, after talking to her supervisor, was flattered to find that it was indeed suitable material.

She spent a day in the library looking through law journals making notes about the types of article they published, and then annotating the 'notes for authors'. She then arranged a meeting with her supervisor and talked about publishing an article. They agreed to work together with Catherine as the first author. They organised the structure and Catherine edited her thesis down to 5,000 words and gave it to her supervisor. After further editing and another meeting the paper was submitted to what they both agreed was a suitable journal. The paper was accepted four months later by both referees with only minor editing needed.

Discussion points

1. What do you think you would get out of publishing your research?
2. Do you know of a journal which is exactly right for the research area you are interested in? If so, what is its title?
3. How important do you think it is to get the format of your article exactly as the publisher wants it? What will happen if you don't?

Questions and answers

Q. *My supervisor doesn't think that there is sufficient novel material in my thesis to warrant its publication in a peer review journal, but I really want to carry on in academia and I need to start publishing for my career. What should I do?*

At this stage you should try to get a second opinion from another member of staff. Your best approach is not to do this behind your supervisor's back, rather mention your worries and why you want to publish and then ask for help. Also ask if they feel that it is a good idea to ask someone else.

Q. *I've had comments back from two referees on my article – one of them felt that it was OK and just needed a few small problems sorting out, the other thought that the research area was not within the remit of the journal and for that reason should be rejected. What do I do?*

Look on the bright side – neither referee has said your research isn't up to scratch! The best thing to do is to talk to your supervisor about what has happened. It is often possible to simply make some changes which alter the emphasis of your article so that it does fit within the remit of the journal – this does not change your research, or mean you have to do more research. It usually won't mean that you need to find another journal, although the final decision will be at the discretion of the editor.

Q. *My supervisor is pushing me to publish the research, but I've just started a job in an unrelated field and I'm really short of time. I can't see any value for my career in publishing. What do I say to my supervisor?*

One possibility is to suggest that the supervisor prepares a paper for publication. Explain that you are too busy at present but would be happy to co-author a paper if the supervisor is prepared to find the appropriate journal and carry out all the required editing. You will need to discuss who should be the first-named author as this is quite important for prestige. It really should be you because it is your research and the supervisor is not likely to spend anything like the amount of time in editing your work that you put into the research. If more research is required this situation may change.

Glossary

Attitudinal data an attitude is the tendency to evaluate something in a particular way. Attitudinal data present measures of such evaluations and can come in several different forms – rated numerically or along various scales.

Bibliography the complete list of full publication details appended to a thesis. Not all of these may be cited in the text.

BIDS/ISI, OCLC FirstSearch databases of journal articles available through the Internet. Full text can be downloaded.

Bookmark an Internet browser facility which helps you to find the same page again quickly.

Citation bibliographic material acknowledging the work of another person. In the Harvard system the author's name and the date of publication are inserted in brackets at the point in the text where the quotation occurs.

Code of practice institutional statement of the standards and procedures expected or required of both students and of supervisors and departments.

Confidential communication a communication between parties who stand in a confidential relationship with each other, and which the law protects.

Draft a version of the written-up account of research (either in full or part); usually a first or earlier version, as distinct from a 'final draft'.

Edit	careful perusal of text to be sure that it makes sense and is consistent. Changes should be made to improve the precision and readability.
Empiricism	an approach that advocates experience and observation to support knowledge claims.
Epistemology	the grounds for knowledge claims.
Extensive research	research which looks for regularities and patterns within a broad population.
Focus group	small group of people. Interviews (unstructured) with these make use of group dynamics to stimulate discussion. These are carried out not only to ascertain the group's views, but also to examine the dynamics within the group.
Generic skills	skills expected or required, generally at a certain level of activity as distinct from the more specialised skills appropriate for a narrower area of activity. In the context of research, for instance, design and planning skills, communication and writing skills, and information technology skills would usually be classed as generic, as being necessary for any kind of research activity.
Headed paper	paper with the official logo or address of an institution or an organisation. It can be obtained for your institution by your thesis supervisor and will help give your research enquiries an 'official stamp'.
Inspiration	software which enables the user to create diagrams of ideas and concepts.

	Outlines of mind maps can also be derived by the software.
Intensive research	research which concentrates on a particular case, or on a small number of cases, and seeks to address why and how specific sets of events and processes occur.
Interpretative (also known as **hermeneutics**)	an approach to social science that stresses the symbolic and meaningful aspects of social behaviour.
Interview schedule	a list of topics, or even complete questions, which can be used as to guide the order and nature of questions in an interview.
JANET (Joint Academic Network)	connection to other academic libraries is possible via the Internet through your own library catalogue.
Libertas	one of the on-line public assess systems (OPACS) used in academic libraries. It includes the catalogue, your own use of the library and access to JANET.
Literature	a term often used to indicate the secondary written sources for a particular subject, usually located in a library and comprising descriptive, critical or analytical commentary and discussion, frequently in the format of monographs and journal articles.
Master's degree	generally indicating the first level of postgraduate degree study. In the UK a Master's degree may be based on a taught programme of studies, or based purely on research. In the latter case it is usually designated as an MPhil degree.

Method/methodology the way in which research is carried out and sources used. For instance library-based research uses material and data located in libraries; fieldwork gathers information from the actual situation being discussed in the research, for example asking questions of the people whose situation or behaviour is being investigated.

Methodology the critical analysis of methods.

Mind map a note-taking technique promoted by Tony Buzan. Diagramming is used to show relationships between concepts and their components.

Ontology an account of the phenomena under study and the relationships between these phenomena.

Paragraph a group of sentences that introduces an aspect of an idea/argument/procedure. It defines, gives examples and develops the topic, and then brings all to a conclusion. A link to the next aspect or topic may be included. Paragraphs may contain up to ten sentences or as few as two. One-sentence paragraphs are not very helpful.

Parallel construction sentence construction which follows the same format for a series of aspects in order to display the equality of relationship they all bear to the subject of the sentence or its verb. Lists or bullet points all need to begin with the same form of word: nouns, gerunds, infinitives or active verbs.

Plagiarism copying words written by another person without acknowledgement.

This practice is viewed with grave concern in the academic community.

Population   this refers to the unit or elements being studied. It need not be 'the population' as traditionally understood, in terms of individuals living within a particular area, but can refer to any collection of items under research; for example a group of hospitals, a number of local authorities or a collection of shops

Positivism   a philosophy of science and social science that stresses empirical support and the generation of general laws to explain phenomena.

Project   a particular research activity or programme.

Proof-read   reading a draft which is ready for submission to catch and correct mechanical errors of spelling, punctuation and formatting.

Qualitative data   data which are non-numeric in form, usually focusing on people's beliefs, values and meanings.

Quantitative data   data which are numeric and can be counted and quantified.

Rationalism   an approach to knowledge production using faculties of reasoning.

Reference   references are the full list of actual texts cited. Full publication details must be included.

Register   the level of language represented by the preciseness of the vocabulary. Spoken registers are informal and include slang, conversational, colloquial and dialectal English. Written registers are formal and include, academic, professional and specialist language.

Regulations   precisely drafted and formal requirements relating to the programme of studies and process of assessment used for the award of a degree.

Respondents   the sources of your research information. They provide the data which you analyse and interpret.

Sampling   the method through which a population is reduced in size to manageable research proportions.

Sampling frame   the list of population members from which the sample is drawn. Ideally it should contain a complete listing of every element in the target population.

Submission   handing over finally a completed piece of work, for instance a thesis, for purposes of examination for the award of the degree.

Subordination   a way of showing that information is less important than the main idea but is, nevertheless, related to or has some effect on the main idea. A subordinated idea occurs in a clause which begins with words such as 'since', 'when', 'because', 'until', 'which' and 'that'.

Supervisor   a member of the academic staff in a university or other higher education institution assigned to advise and monitor the progress of a student carrying out research for a degree.

Theory	a logically interrelated set of abstractions, ideas and propositions about empirical reality that organises knowledge about the world.
Thesis	a written account of research submitted for the award of a postgraduate degree. The word is also used in a wider sense to refer to an argument or theory put forward in an academic context.
Thesis statement	a clear statement of the scope and parameters of an investigation, what factors limit those parameters, how the thesis is organised and what methods will be employed to reach a conclusion.
Transcript	the word-by-word written recording of an interview from a recorded tape, usually typed to facilitate further analysis.
Transition words	words which link one part of a sentence to another, one sentence to another or paragraphs to each other. Included in this type are words such as 'hence', 'therefore', 'moreover' and 'nevertheless'.
Triangulation	the use of multiple research methods and sources of data to cross-check individual accounts and build up a body of evidence.
Web search engine	a search and index service which are very useful paths to finding information more easily on the Internet. Examples include Alta-Vista, Google, Infoseek, Lycos and Yahoo!

Widows and orphans a term used to identify parts of word-processed text. If one line of a list (or a title of a section) is left at the bottom of a page, it is called a widow. If one line of a list is left at the top of a page, it is called an orphan.

Index

academic, 2–3, 5, 7, 14, 69, 71–2,
74, 86–7, 105, 107, 114,
116–17, 127, 129–31
administrator, 103
agenda, 37
agreement, 78, 92
aide-mémoire, 8
aims, 17, 32, 51, 56, 74, 85, 99,
114
analyse, 19, 31, 40, 42–3, 51, 56,
63–4, 74, 95, 128, 130–1
appeal, 107–8, 110
article, 51, 70, 86, 95, 114–15,
117–21, 123–4
assessment, 21, 53, 59, 64, 90, 99,
107, 130
attitudinal data, 34, 131

bibliography, 9, 11, 69–71, 79, 81,
95, 125
bookmark, 69, 125
brainstorm, 72–4, 81

caption, 102
catalogue, 69, 127
chapters, 1, 9, 17, 19, 29, 44,
51–2, 56, 75, 81, 85–6, 88, 90,
95, 97, 99, 103, 113, 115
citation, 79, 87, 90, 125
code of practice, 14, 125
cohesion, 74–6
colleague, 69, 116
communication, 125–6
conciseness, 74, 76
conclusions, 18–19, 45, 52, 54, 56,
59–60, 74, 80, 82, 128, 131
confidentiality, 15, 85, 91–4,
96–7, 125
copyright, 85–90, 95–7, 115
correlation, 61, 63–4
course director, 103
critical, 19, 21, 32, 68–9, 127–8

deadline, 4–5, 67, 80, 95, 101,
104–6, 108–10, 120, 122

degree, 2, 10–11, 14–15, 62, 82,
103–7, 113, 127, 130–1
dissertation, 1, 27, 110–11
documents, 39–40, 42–3, 47, 69,
79, 81
domain, 52–3, 92, 97
draft, 9–12, 74, 77–8, 80–1,
109–10, 115, 122, 125–6, 129
Duration of Copyright
Regulations, 88

economic rights, 86
edit, 77, 115, 121–2, 126
editors, 72, 117, 119, 122, 124
effective, 33, 70
electronic database, 69, 125
empiricism, 19, 22, 51, 54, 126,
129, 131
epistemology, 19, 21–3, 25,
126
equality, 57–8, 61, 128
ethics, 26, 93–4, 96–7
evaluation, 18, 22, 73, 120, 125
examination, 12, 29, 62, 78,
103–5, 107–8, 111–12, 130
examiner, 90, 103–5, 107, 110,
112, 122
extensive, 30–1, 34, 92, 126
external examiner, 103, 105, 107,
112

failure, 18, 71, 99, 107–8
focus group, 35, 37, 126
font, 102
footnotes, 95, 102
format, 6, 33, 71, 74, 77, 80, 82,
99–101, 105, 109–10, 113, 117,
119, 122–3, 127–9
function, 52–3, 56–7, 60–1

generic, 2, 126
glossary, 103
grammar, 77, 82
group, 35–7, 46–7, 54, 56–8,
60–1, 64, 112, 126, 128–9

headed paper, 45, 126
hermeneutics, 127

independent, 2–3, 11, 15, 21, 105
inspiration, 73, 126
intensive, 30–2, 127
internal examiner, 104, 110
Internet, 69, 79, 85, 87, 94, 125, 127, 131
interpretative, 23–5, 127
intervals, 44, 57–64
interview, 12, 21, 33–6, 42–3, 45–6, 48, 85, 91–3, 96, 106, 127, 131

JANET, 69, 127
journal, 72, 81–2, 114–25, 127

length, 2, 6, 13, 40, 47–8, 51–2, 68, 71, 80–1, 87–8, 101–2, 110, 113, 115, 122
Libertas, 69, 127
line spacing, 102, 119
linear, 43, 56–8, 60–1
literary works, 87
literature, 6, 9, 39, 71, 82, 127

magazine, 115
margins, 102
Master's, 3, 5, 29, 113–14, 116, 121–2, 127
mean, 20, 23, 27, 31, 41, 55, 59–62, 64, 79, 92, 97, 112, 114, 116, 119, 124
measurements, 51–9, 61–2, 64
media, 39
median, 61, 64
method, 5, 10, 30, 32–4, 37, 41, 55, 128, 130
methodology, 2, 9, 11–12, 19, 21, 128
mind map, 73, 81, 127–8
mode, 61, 64, 69, 95
MPhil, 2, 127

nominal, 44, 57–8, 61, 63–4
notes for authors, 117–19, 123
numerals, 52

objective, 23
objectives, 1, 6, 8–9, 11, 13, 18, 23, 30
observation, 22, 24, 33, 37–8, 126
ontology, 19–21, 23, 128
order, 7, 14, 24, 34–5, 43, 45, 48, 52, 57, 59, 61, 64, 69, 73, 77, 79, 82, 89, 103, 117, 121, 127–8
ordinal, 44, 57–8, 60–4

panels, 95
paragraph, 74–6, 128
parallel construction, 75, 79, 128
participation, 33, 37–8
peer review, 114–16, 123
percentiles, 61
permitted acts, 86, 89
permutation, 57–8, 61
PhD, 2, 62, 95
phenomena, 18–20, 24, 26, 40, 54, 128–9
philosophy, 20–2, 27, 129
planning, 1–2, 9, 46, 72, 74, 81, 117, 126
politics, 26, 37
population, 31, 34, 41, 48, 126, 129–30
positivism, 23, 129
postgraduate, 1–2, 15, 127, 131
procrastinate, 68
product moment correlation, 61, 63–4
project, 3, 5, 8–10, 13, 18, 30, 45, 102, 129
proof-read, 77–81, 129
publishers, 88, 90, 113, 115, 117, 123
punctuation, 77–8, 80, 128–9

qualitative, 2, 29–34, 37, 39, 41–4, 47, 129

quantitative, 23, 29–30, 32–4, 44, 47, 51, 56, 129
question, 5, 7, 18, 22, 25, 27, 30–1, 34, 42, 48, 53, 91, 93, 97, 112
questionnaire, 30–1, 33–5, 42, 46–8, 85, 91–2

range, 27, 32–4, 37, 39–40, 45–6, 52–3
ratio, 44, 57–8, 60–4
rationalism, 22, 129
referees, 114, 119–24
reference, 21, 40, 71, 80, 82, 90, 95, 129
register, 77, 82, 129
regulations, 2, 5, 10, 71, 74, 88, 101–2, 105, 109–11, 130
research, 1–11, 13–15, 17–27, 29–34, 37, 39–43, 45, 47–8, 51, 54, 56, 69, 74, 77, 80, 82, 85–6, 89, 91–5, 99–100, 103, 105–6, 110, 113–17, 120–31
respondents, 34, 41–2, 45, 48, 130
risk, 14, 52
rules, 6, 39, 48, 51–9, 62, 70, 87–8, 93, 100

sampling, 31, 34, 41, 45, 48, 72, 130
Sampling, 41
scales, 2, 5, 30–1, 33, 47, 51, 56–64, 131
schedule, 35, 46, 99, 109, 127
search engine, 69, 131
similarity, 31, 57–8, 60–1

skills, 2, 13, 67, 126
statistics, 23, 32, 60–2
study, 1–3, 14, 18–24, 26–7, 31, 37, 39, 48, 70, 86, 89, 114, 127–8
submission, 5, 11, 78, 99–101, 103–4, 106, 108–11, 115, 122, 129–30
subordination, 76, 130
summary, 9, 37, 60, 90, 103, 118
supervisor, 1–6, 9–15, 26–7, 62–3, 69, 77–82, 90, 94–5, 97, 101–5, 107–11, 113, 115, 117, 121–4, 126, 130
survey, 31, 34, 41, 46–7, 68

taxonomy, 31
temperature, 53–7, 59
theory, 17–21, 23–7, 131
thesis, 1–7, 9–15, 29–30, 32, 45, 47, 51, 62, 68–9, 72–4, 77–8, 81–3, 85–6, 92, 94–5, 99–113, 121–3, 125–6, 130–1
transcript, 43, 48, 131
transformation, 56–7, 59
transition, 76, 131
triangulation, 46, 131
typeface, 102

undergraduate, 1–2

variance, 60–1
viva voce, 104, 106, 111–12

widows and orphans, 80, 132